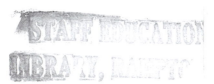

THE MAUDSLEY

Maudsley Monographs

MAUDSLEY MONOGRAPHS

HENRY MAUDSLEY, from whom the series of monographs takes its name, was the founder of The Maudsley Hospital and the most prominent English psychiatrist of his generation. The Maudsley Hospital was united with the Bethlem Royal Hospital in 1948 and its medical school, renamed the Institute of Psychiatry at the same time, became a constituent part of the British Postgraduate Medical Federation. It is now associated with King's College, London, and entrusted with the duty of advancing psychiatry by teaching and research. The Bethlem-Maudsley NHS Trust, together with the Institute of Psychiatry, are jointly known as The Maudsley.

The monograph series reports work carried out at The Maudsley. Some of the monographs are directly concerned with clinical problems; others, less obviously relevant, are in scientific fields that are cultivated for the furtherance of psychiatry.

Editor
Professor David P Goldberg MA DM MSc FRCP FRCPsych DPM
Assistant Editors
Dr A S David MPhil MSc FRCP MRCPsych MD
Dr T Wykes BSc PhD MPhil

Previous Editors

1955-1962	Professor Sir Aubrey Lewis LLD DSc MD FRCP and Professor G W Harris MA MD DSc FRS
1962-1966	Professor Sir Aubrey Lewis LLD DSc MD FRCP
1966-1970	Professor Sir Denis Hill MB FRCP FRCPsych DPM and Professor J T Eayrs PhD DSc
1970-1979	Professor Sir Denis Hill MB FRCP FRCPsych DPM and Professor G S Brindley MD FRCP FRS
1979-1981	Professor G S Brindley MD FRCP FRS and Professor G F M Russell MD FRCP FRCP(ED) FRCPsych
1981-1983	Professor G F M Russell MD FRCP FRCP(ED) FRCPsych
1983-1989	Professor G F M Russell MD FRCP FRCP(ED) FRCPsych and Professor E Marley MA MD DSc FRCP FRCPsych DPM
1989-1993	Professor G F M Russell MD FRCP FRCP(ED) FRCPsych and Professor B H Anderton BSc PhD

Maudsley Monographs number thirty-eight

Fitness to Plead in England and Wales

Don Grubin MD MRCPsych
University of Newcastle

Psychology Press
An imprint of Erlbaum (UK) Taylor & Francis

Copyright © 1996 by Psychology Press
an imprint of Erlbaum (UK) Taylor & Francis Ltd.

Psychology Press, Publishers
27 Church Road
Hove
East Sussex, BN3 2FA
UK

British Library Cataloguing in Publication Data

A catalogue record for this book is available from the British Library

ISBN 0-86377-424-5
ISSN 0076-5465

Printed and bound by TJ Press (Padstow) Ltd.

Contents

Acknowledgements

Most of the data collection for this study took place while I was a research registrar at the Maudsley Hospital in a post funded by the Wellcome Foundation, to whom a great deal of thanks are due. In addition I would like to thank Professor John Gunn of the Institute of Psychiatry for his support and supervision, and indeed for making the study possible in the first place. I am also very grateful to Dr Graham Robertson of the Institute of Psychiatry for his computer expertise, for his sound artistic and design advice, and for helping me over a number of conceptual hurdles. At the Home Office, Mr Robert Baxter and all of his colleagues in C3 Division offered an exceptional amount of co-operation; Mr Andy Pickersgill in particular ensured that the research ran smoothly. Though I benefited from the many discussions I had at the Home Office, all of the opinions expressed here are of course my own, and in no way reflect either official or unofficial Home Office thinking. Finally, I would like to thank my 3-year-old son, Oliver, who helped with some of the typing.

Abstract

The concept of being fit to plead to a criminal charge is fundamental to British law and to those legal systems that have evolved from it. However, the procedure by which an individual is found unfit to plead, together with the consequences that flow from that decision, have been criticised frequently. Despite the medical, legal, and ethical concerns that have been expressed about the finding, discussion of the issues has taken place in a factual vacuum, with little research having been carried out in relation to the concept in England and Wales.

In this study, the development of the concept is traced from its antecedents in medieval England to its modern form. It is argued that the mentally ill and the mentally defective have been mistakenly linked together in respect of the notion, with important consequences for its use in the 20th century.

In order to understand how the concept of fitness to plead is applied and the effects it has on mentally disordered defendants, the Home Office files of all 295 defendants found unfit to plead between 1976 and 1988 were evaluated. It was found that approximately 60% of the defendants suffered from schizophrenia and a quarter were mentally handicapped. Just over 25% of the alleged offences were of a serious nature, and in more than 80% of cases the evidence linking the accused with the offence appeared to be strong. Nearly half of the sample (46%) recovered their fitness to plead; of these, about 80% did so within a year of the finding. Seventy-six individuals (26%) returned for trial, while 68 (23%) were still in hospital at the end of the survey period.

Problems with the working of the law in relation to fitness to plead are discussed, recent changes in the law are critically reviewed, and recommendations for reform are made. In particular, it is argued that consideration of the issue should be a last resort and more firmly focused on the issue of a fair trial in cases where guilt is in doubt, on the grounds that a trial in the presence of a competent defendant is to be preferred to a "trial of facts" in a defendant's absence.

Specifically, it is recommended that fitness to plead should be decided in all cases by a judge, rather than by a jury as at present, based on a consideration of the facts of the case where guilt is unclear; that in cases of mental illness, once the issue of fitness to plead is raised but before a finding is reached, there should be a mandatory treatment period of up to one year; that in the event of an unfitness finding and a trial of the facts of the case, a "guilty" verdict should be recorded as "a finding of unfit to plead *and* proven", whereas a "*not* guilty" finding should be recorded as a plain acquittal; and that in cases of "unfit to plead *and* proven", the judge should set a time period over which, if the patient's mental state improves and he or she contests the verdict, a trial will be held.

CHAPTER ONE

Introduction

The concept of being fit to plead to a criminal charge is fundamental to British law and to those legal systems that have evolved from it. It arises from the notion that it is against natural justice to bring to trial those of unsound mind who cannot plead with understanding to the charges brought against them. Formed from legal bricks and psychiatric mortar in the 19th century but built on foundations first laid in the Middle Ages, the concept of fitness to plead has been only partly modernised in the 20th century; though subject to numerous changes and putative improvements over the years, it remains in essence a Victorian edifice. As might be expected for such an ersatz structure bound together by a somewhat unstable mixture of law and psychiatry, it is not viewed with complete contentment by either lawyers or psychiatrists, and the procedure by which an individual is found unfit to plead, together with the consequences that flow from such a decision, have been criticised frequently (Chiswick, 1990a; Emmins, 1986; Gostin, 1986; Grubin, 1991a; Home Office & DHSS, 1975). Considerable unease has been expressed on clinical, ethical, and practical grounds to the extent that it has been referred to in the Court of Appeal by Lord Justice Sachs as "this much dreaded order" (R v *Webb*, 1969, p.628), which is perhaps not what one would expect for a procedure that is supposed to function in the interests of the mentally disordered defendant.

A person is found unfit to plead if he or she fails to satisfy criteria first enunciated in R v *Dyson* (1831) but more fully described by Baron

1

Alderson in R v *Pritchard* (1836). The basic issue was defined as being whether a defendant was of *sufficient intellect* to make a proper defence. This has been interpreted as the defendant being able to plead to the indictment, to comprehend the details of evidence and the course of proceedings, and to know that a juror can be challenged. More recently, the ability to instruct legal advisers has also been included (Mitchell & Richardson, 1985). Since the 19th century, a person found unfit to plead was considered to be insane on arraignment and subject to the provisions of the Criminal Lunatics Act 1800. Though the legal processing of those found unfit to plead has since been modified by the Criminal Procedure (Insanity) Act 1964, and more recently by the Criminal Procedure (Insanity and Unfitness to Plead) Act 1991, the legal equivalence of a finding of unfitness to plead and insanity, and the emphasis on intellectual ability in favour of other components of the mental state, have remained unchanged.

The research described here was undertaken when the Criminal Procedure (Insanity) Act 1964 (CP(I)A) was the operative law in relation to those found unfit to plead. This Act required that those found "under disability" in relation to trial (i.e. unfit to plead) should be admitted to hospital under conditions that became equivalent to sections 37 and 41 of the Mental Health Act 1983, that is, a hospital order with Home Office restrictions on discharge without limit of time. If the patient became fit to plead, the Act allowed for remission back to court at the discretion of the Secretary of State; a patient who was not remitted for trial or who did not become fit to plead remained in hospital on the same basis as any patient detained under a restriction order, with discharge by the Secretary of State or a Mental Health Review Tribunal dependent on clinical and public safety considerations.

The provisions of the CP(I)A have been perceived as having important negative consequences for those found unfit to plead, discouraging the use of the finding and hence depriving mentally disordered individuals of the protection of one of the basic tenets of British law: the right to a fair trial. The deficiencies of the CP(I)A were particularly well rehearsed in 1975 in the report of the Butler Committee as part of its overall review of the law in relation to the mentally abnormal offender (Home Office & DHSS, 1975). Perhaps the Committee's most serious concern was the fact that those found unfit to plead could be detained in hospital for indefinite periods regardless of their need for treatment, and even if their capacity to plead was restored. In effect, individuals were deprived of their right to trial and faced possible life detention in psychiatric hospital for crimes they were only alleged to have committed. It took 16 years, however, before even a limited number of the Butler recommendations were finally put into effect.

Despite the medical, legal, and ethical concerns that have been expressed about the finding of unfitness to plead, discussion of the issues has taken place in a factual vacuum. Before the research described here was carried out and made available to the Home Office (some of which has now been published: Grubin, 1991a,b,c), the research literature on unfitness to plead in England and Wales was limited to one study, a survey of psychiatric reports prepared at the time of trial for patients in one English special hospital (Larkin & Collins, 1989). Extending the net to Scotland increased the corpus by only two more studies, one based on patients in a Scottish special hospital (Chiswick, 1978), the other a review of Scottish murder cases that eventually returned for trial (Normand, 1984). Nor was it straightforward to determine the number of people who were actually found unfit to plead: Since 1980 the figures for England and Wales have been combined with insanity verdicts, and enquiries about the number of cases before that year revealed frequent discrepancies between the data published by HMSO in *Criminal Statistics for England and Wales* and internal Home Office figures (Grubin, unpublished). Thus, even the thorough review carried out by the Butler Committee had to depend primarily on the impressions of those dealing with unfit to plead cases rather than on facts culled from systematic research (Home Office & DHSS, 1975).

The research reported here was designed therefore to look in detail at how the law in relation to unfitness to plead affects the mentally disordered defendant; it involved examination of the cases of all individuals found unfit to plead in the 13-year period 1976 to 1988. The main question the research set out to answer was whether the law has had its desired effect: the protection of the mentally disordered defendant from the distress of a court appearance and the risks of an unfair trial. However, the research also addressed the subsidiary question of whether being found unfit to plead actually works in the interests of the mentally disordered, or whether the risk of an unfair trial may in fact be a more preferable option. Linked to this issue is the question of how the changes in law brought about by the Criminal Procedure (Insanity and Unfitness to Plead) Act 1991 are likely to affect the mentally disordered defendant. Finally, from a more theoretical perspective, the research will be applied to the question of just how comfortably this Victorian structure sits within the environment of modern medicolegal concepts.

CHAPTER TWO

Historical background and legislation

Although fitness to plead is associated with the concepts of a fair trial and the protection of the mentally disordered defendant from the rigours of a court appearance, its origins lie in the procedural formalities of the medieval court of law: Without the opening plea and the accused's consent to trial by jury, the trial could not take place. As Walker points out in his historical review of crime and insanity (Walker, 1968, p.220), "For medieval and Tudor judges … the commonest difficulty with which they had to contend at the outset of a trial for felony or treason was presented by the man who simply refused to plead 'guilty' or 'not guilty'. Unless he uttered the necessary words, reverence for the ritual of the law made it unthinkable to proceed with the trial, with the result that he could not be convicted and executed". Thus, those who could not, and those who would not, offer a plea to the court posed a similar problem for an adversarial process that required the accused to respond to allegations made against him, and for the early courts of England three types of individual became closely linked: the insane, the deaf-mute, and the individual who, for more calculated reasons, decided it was not in his best interests to enter a plea. The distinction between "mute of malice" and "mute by visitation of God" thus became entwined with court procedure and fitness to plead from the origins of modern legal processes. But in order to understand fully how this situation came about and how it continued to evolve, it is necessary to review first the early relationship between the mentally abnormal and the law.

ANGLO-SAXON AND NORMAN ANTECEDENTS

Generalisations about the legal framework of pre-Norman England can be made only with caution as different localities had diverse customs, with a network of competing courts covering the country (Holdsworth, 1922). Walker (1968) refers to the transcription of a text ascribed to Egbert, Archbishop of York in the 8th century, which outlines the state of law in pre-Norman Northumbria, and though it is unclear how representative this is of Anglo-Saxon England in general, it appears similar at least to the 7th-century Kent of King Aethelberht (Richardson & Sayles, 1966). In both Northumbria and Kent crime was a matter for compensation for loss of property, injury, or loss of life, rather than for trial and sentence in any formal sense, with a failure to pay compensation resulting in a blood feud between the families of victim and offender. The amount of compensation payable depended on the nature and severity of the injury, and on the status of offender and victim. The rules were similar and equally clear in the case of the insane, with Egbert writing: "If a man fall out of his senses or wits, and it come to pass that he kill someone, let his kinsmen pay for the victim . . ." (Thorpe, 1840, quoted in Walker, 1968, p.15).

Notions of intent, *mens rea*, and responsibility were not relevant, though to some extent they were recognised (for instance, Church as opposed to secular law demanded different penances depending on whether a homicide was accidental or premeditated); it was the committal of the act itself that was the primary concern. By the time of the Norman Conquest, however, a number of crimes such as murder, arson, adultery, and treachery against one's lord had become public wrongs and could no longer be put right by simple compensation, and were instead punishable by death or mutilation and the expropriation of the offender's property by the Crown. Guilt, when in doubt, could be determined by the Deity through the trial by ordeal, which was then followed by the relevant punishment. For a slave this meant ordeal by water, which required the accused, with bandaged hand, to put his arm into a bowl of boiling water up to the wrist, or if subject to the "triple ordeal" up to the elbow, to pick up a stone at the bottom of the bowl; after three days the bandages were removed, and if the arm was scalded, guilt was declared. Alternatives for the freeman involved ordeal by hot iron, which required him to walk over red-hot ploughshares without being scarred, to put his hand into a glove of hot iron, or to pick up a red-hot iron bar and hold it in his bare hand; again, the presence of blisters in three day's time was a sign of guilt (Hibbert, 1963; Richardson & Sayles, 1966).

The primacy of the *actus reus* remained overriding into the 13th century, but the relevance of intention was becoming increasingly acknowledged. The 10th-century laws of both Aethelred and his successor Cnut, for example, stated that those who committed a misdeed involuntarily or unintentionally should be "entitled to clemency" (Walker, 1968). It is not clear from these laws how the insane or the mentally defective were to be dealt with, but local custom probably ensured that they were not brought to trial in the first place, at least to the court of the king. The *Laws of Henry the First*, for instance, give a good account of both custom and law in southern England around the time of the Norman conquest. In the *Laws* it is stated that "Insane persons and evildoers of a like sort should be guarded and treated leniently by their parents" (quoted in Walker, 1968, p.17), though it should be noted that their families were still expected to pay compensation.

By the 11th century trial by ordeal and other methods of determining guilt such as compurgation (in which a number of compurgators or witnesses swore to the good character and innocence of the accused) and trial by combat (in which the accused might establish his innocence by challenging his accuser to a duel) became less accepted, and the king's courts started to replace them (Holdsworth, 1922; Turner, 1968). During the reign of Henry II in the late 12th century, a system of prosecution by the Crown was established in which trials for serious offences were conducted by travelling justices, the offender having been first "declared" by the hundred jury (a forerunner of the modern grand jury). In the early 13th century the petty jury supplanted the trial by ordeal, which was finally abolished following the Lateran Council of 1215. Perhaps under the influence of Roman law, and with the Crown becoming both more powerful and intent on consolidating its power, serious crimes were no longer simply matters for compensation, but were seen as crimes against society, which the king was entitled to punish (Hibbert, 1963).

Thus, by the 1200s it had become the practice for juries to determine both whether a defendant should be tried and whether he was guilty or innocent. These developments had the effect of bringing insane and mentally defective offenders into the sphere of the court. Whereas previously the mentally disordered might simply have been confined in prison by the sheriff or released into the protection of their families, now they had to be tried (Walker, 1968, pp.19–20): "The usual procedure was for the jury to certify the facts and for the king to decide what should be done with the [insane] offender. . . . The king must be consulted not because the jury or justices were at a loss but because it was not for them to interfere with the normal course of the law by excusing him from the automatic penalty for his felony". Indeed, Walker describes how in 1293 justices in Cumberland were fined for releasing on their own authority a madman who had been convicted of arson, as only the king could divert the due process of law. And though the king might show leniency or even pardon the insane, it was not until the early 16th century that cases began to appear regularly in which the insane were actually acquitted of their crimes (Walker, 1968).

But what did madness mean in 13th- and 14th-century England, the time when the concept of being fit to plead began to develop? Certainly in terms of the civil law the difference between idiocy (natural fools) and madness (the lunatic) was well recognised, the former existing from birth and considered a permanent condition, the latter of later onset and involving fits of madness but where recovery was possible. The distinction was important in relation to the laws of Chancery, for though the Crown assumed the responsibility for administering the estates of both madman and idiot, it was entitled to take profits for itself only from the estates of idiots, which it looked after for the life of the individual; feudal law had little interest in the idiot or madman who did not have property ("Comment", 1951; Holdsworth, 1922).

In the case of the idiot, "diagnosis" was based on intelligence, which is clear from this somewhat later, mid-16th-century definition (Fitz-Herbert, *Natura brevium,* quoted in "Comment", 1951, p.363):

> And he who shall be said to be a Sot and Idiot from his birth, is such a Person who cannot account or number twenty Pence, nor can tell who his Father or Mother is, nor how old he is &c, so as it may appear that he hath no Understanding or Reason what shall be for his Profit and what for his Loss: But if he hath such Understanding that he know and understand his Letters, & do read by Teaching or Information of Another man, then it seemeth he is not a Sot nor a natural Idiot . . .

In the case of the insane, however, the situation was more complicated. Bracton, one of the first English legal writers to consider the topic in detail, provides a useful insight into contemporary thinking on the meaning of insanity. Bracton believed that the madman was not responsible for his acts, being protected by "the misfortune of his deed. In misdeeds we look to the will and not the outcome. . . ." (quoted in Walker, 1968, p.26; Walker suggests that this may be a misquotation of the Roman writer Modestinus who referred to "the misfortune of his fate"). Madmen, for Bracton, were totally lacking in "discretion", and "are not very different from animals who lack understanding" (quoted in Walker, 1968, p.28), not being able to understand the nature of their acts and thus being unable to form the necessary intention to be guilty of a crime. But the degree of insanity in the accused needed to be considerable: There had to be a *total* lack of discretion, and Bracton's frequent use of the term *furiosus* suggests that he had in mind violent, raving behaviour. His choice of words is suggestive, at least to the 20th-century reader, that more than simple rationality may have been involved, but his ideas (which were probably not original to him) became incorporated in the "wild beast test" of insanity used in the years before McNaughton, in which it was the total deprivation of reason rather than any other abnormal mental or emotional state that defined how the law identified the insane.

It was with the coming together of two streams, therefore—one demanding that the formalities of court procedure be followed, the other defining insanity in terms of rationality—that provided the basis for what was to become the modern notion of fitness to plead. Prior to the 13th century, it was unusual for the madman, the deaf-mute, or the idiot to be brought to trial, though the serious offender might have been locked up by those responsible for law enforcement; after this time the three sailed in the same boat, with rationality acting as the rudder which would steer them into trial, or onto the rocks of a now more formalised indefinite containment awaiting the King's Pleasure.

MEDIEVAL ORIGINS

Though the idea of being unfit to plead as we know it did not take shape until the 19th century, its seeds and early growth can be clearly recognised as early as the 14th century. Until then, as described above, the insane, the idiot, and the deaf-mute might have been informally diverted from trial, but once the system of presenting the accused to the court by the hundred jury became the norm, a more formal method needed to be found. The first clear example of the courts having to deal with such a case is referred to by Walker (1968), who notes a discussion between the itinerant justices of Edward III in 1353 in which one mentions the case of a man who killed four people when "enrage". The justice did not try the man, but remanded him to prison with the intention of bringing him back to trial once he had recovered. In the event the man was never tried, but was pardoned by the king.

The necessity of the plea for the ritual start of the trial has already been referred to in the opening of this chapter. But the individual accused of a serious offence who did not present a plea did more than just inhibit the demands of justice and interfere with the smooth running of the legal process. Without a trial and finding of guilt, the property of the offender could not be expropriated by the Crown. In order to overcome these difficulties created by the defendant who would not plead, recalcitrant individuals were given three warnings, and then confined in a narrow cell and starved until they either reconsidered their positions or died, a technique called the *prison forte et dure* (Griffiths, 1884; Pike, 1873); from 1406, however, withholding of food was replaced by the *peine forte et dure* in which the mute prisoner was both starved and gradually crushed under increasing weights, again until he was either dead or had agreed to enter a plea. Hale, in *The history of the pleas of the Crown* (Hale, 1971, Vol. ii, p.319), gives a good account of what was involved:

> [The prisoner shall be] put into a dark, lower room, and there to be laid naked on the bare ground upon his back without any clothes or rushes under him or to cover him except his privy members, his legs and arms drawn and extended with cords to the four corners of the room, and upon his body laid as great a weight of iron, as he can bear, and more. And the first day he shall have three morsels of barley bread without drink, the second day he shall have three draughts of water, of standing water next the door of the prison, without bread, and this to be his diet till he die.

Hale goes on to say that "tho sometimes it hath been given and executed, yet for the most part men bethink themselves and plead". Griffiths (1884) describes the case of two highway robbers who in 1723 were confronted with the press after they refused to plead: One, on seeing it, asked to be returned to court so that he could plead, "a favour that was granted him, it might have been denied"; the other was put under the press where he withstood a weight of 350 pounds for over half an hour, but on the addition of 50 more pounds he too begged to plead. Both were convicted and hanged. There was a different outcome in the case of a Major Strangeways in 1658 whose attendants in pity added their own weights to his load so that "they might sooner release his soul".

Before resorting to this extreme practice, the court needed to decide whether the defendant who did not reply when asked to plead was mute of malice, in which case he was subjected to the *peine forte et dure*, or mute by the visitation of God and hence spared the *peine*, with a plea of not guilty entered on his behalf on the assumption that this was how he would have pleaded had he been able. But the courts often needed some convincing that "visitation" was genuine, and it was usually the practice to try first to persuade the prisoner to plead by tying his thumbs together with whipcord (Hale, 1971). Pike recounts the following exchange involving a deaf man who would not plead at the Old Bailey in 1734 (Pike, 1876, pp.284–285):

Court: If he remains obstinate, he must be pressed.
Whitesides: The Court says you must be pressed if you won't hear.
Prisoner: Ha!
Court: Read the law, but let the executioner first tie his thumbs.
The executioner tied his thumbs together with whipcord ...
Prisoner: My dear Lord, I am deaf as the ground.
Executioner: Guilty or Not Guilty?
Prisoner: My sweet, sugar, precious lord, I am deaf, indeed, and have been so these ten years.
Executioner: Guilty or Not Guilty?
Court: Hold him there a little ... Now loose the cord, and give him a little time to consider of it, but let him know what he must expect if he continues obstinate, for the Court will not be trifled with.

The *peine* itself was last used in 1736, but it was not officially abolished until 1772. After that date, anyone standing mute of malice to charges of felony or piracy was immediately convicted and sentenced as if he had been found guilty by verdict; those who refused to use the correct verbal formula were likewise convicted without trial. It was not until 1827 that a plea of not guilty was also entered for those standing mute of malice as well as for those mute by visitation (Poole, 1968).

In the case of the deaf-mute defendant, if it was decided that he was mute by visitation rather than of malice, the trial could continue based on the *not guilty* plea that had been entered for the defendant, and someone who was able to communicate with the defendant was asked to assist the court. However, because it is only relatively recently that the deaf have received special training in communication, deaf-mutes would often have appeared mentally backward to the courts ("Comment", 1951), and a further decision about suitability for trial had to be made. This was apparent in Hale's detailed description of 17th-century legal practice in relation to idiocy and insanity. For Hale (1971, Vol. i, p.34), a person who was deaf and dumb from birth was:

> ... in presumption of law an ideot, and the rather, because he hath no possibility to understand, what is forbidden by law to be done, or under what penalties: but if it can appear, that he hath the use of understanding, which many of that condition discover by signs to a very great measure, then he may be tried, and suffer judgement and execution, tho great caution is to be used therein.

Hale's views, published posthumously in the 18th century, had an enormous influence on the law for the next 200 years. Based on his authority, a trial of the deaf-mute could take place as long as the court exercised care that the defendant was not mentally defective; in other words, mute by visitation was not an absolute bar for trial. The case of Elizabeth Steel, a deaf woman charged with grand larceny in 1787, is an often quoted precedent in this respect (though there were in fact earlier cases, for instance, R v *Thomas Jones*, 1773). Steel made no plea to the court and was found mute by the visitation of God. There was doubt about what to do next, and she was remanded so that the assembled judges could consider whether she could be tried. Based on Hale's authority, it was decided some months later that the presumption of idiotism "may be repelled" in her case, and that she could be tried. The judge was most sceptical, but the jury found her mute by visitation for a second time, and a plea of "not guilty" was entered on her behalf. She was, however, found guilty and sentenced to seven years transportation (R v *Steel*, 1787).

Although a two-step process in the case of muteness was required— first to make a decision on the cause of muteness and then to make a decision about whether the defendant was of sufficient intelligence to undergo trial—in effect only the first step had to be taken in the case of the insane person who could not plead, or plead sensibly. This is well illustrated by the case of Somervile, referred to by Hale and described in detail by Walker (1968). In 1583 Somervile, in a "frantic humour", became convinced that it was his destiny to free his religion, Catholicism, from persecution, and that to do this he must shoot the Queen. On his way to London he used his sword to attack a number of people. He was arrested, but when brought to court made no reply when asked his plea. The justices had to decide whether his silence was caused by real or pretended madness, but there was as yet no set procedure for them to follow. They proposed an "inquest of office" to be held by 12 jurors who would determine whether or not Somervile's madness was genuine. If found mad, his trial was to be postponed until he recovered his senses; if it was decided that he was feigning he would not undergo the *peine* (as the offence was treason), but would instead be sentenced. Though the result of the inquest is not clear, it seems to have gone against him as he went on to plead guilty, was convicted, and sentenced to beheading (though before the sentence could be carried out he was found dead in his cell, a probable suicide).

The case of Somervile is one of the first recorded examples of a jury being empanelled to decide on the question of insanity pre-trial. Walker points out that it was not modelled on the petty jury that decided outcome in criminal cases, but on those of civil inquests that were held to decide whether a subject was mentally competent to handle his or her own affairs.

Writing more than a century after the Somervile case, Hale made it explicit that trial should be postponed in the case of the insane, and he advised on the procedure to be followed, at least for capital offences (which, it should be noted, constituted a fairly long list at that time) (Hale, 1971, Vol. i, pp.34–35):

> If a man in his sound memory commits a capital offence, and before his arraignment he becomes absolutely mad, he ought not by law to be arraigned during such his phrenzy, but be remitted to prison until that incapacity be removed; the reason is, because he cannot advisedly plead to the indictment; ... even tho the delinquent in his sound mind were examined, and confessed the offence before his arraignment ...
>
> But because there may be great fraud in this matter ... the judge before such respite of trial or judgement may do well to impanel a jury to inquire *ex officio* touching such insanity, and whether it be real or counterfeit.

Like Bracton, Hale's use of the term "absolutely mad" suggests that for him also the required degree of insanity must be extreme.[1] Indeed, according to Walker it was not until the middle of the 18th century that there was any real chance of the insane (as opposed to deaf-mutes) being found unfit for trial, which is about the same time that special verdicts in cases of insanity began to increase. Perhaps the first case in which the modern form of being unfit to plead can be recognised was that of Dyle in 1756 (quoted by Walker, 1968, pp.222–223). Dyle was accused of murder, but he was not thought to be of sound mind. His lawyer found it impossible to take instructions from him, telling the court "I don't think he is capable of attending to or minding the evidence, or remembering it when he has heard it". The jury found him "not of sound mind and memory", and he was not tried, though his fate is unknown.

Walker found a small number of cases similar to that of Dyle's in the Old Bailey Sessions papers from this time. Perhaps the most notable was the case of Frith, who in 1790 threw a stone at a coach in which George III was riding (*Proceedings in the Case of John Frith*, 1790). Arrested for high treason, he was found to be well and truly insane, but he objected strenuously to any postponement of his trial. A jury was therefore empanelled to determine whether he was "in a fit situation to plead". Before the jury he was overinclusive, grandiose, paranoid, and claimed to have powers like St Paul. The Lord Chief Justice, Lord

Kenyon, before whom the case was heard, referred to both English law and natural justice when he told the jury (cols. 317–318):

> ... the humanity of the law of England falling into that which common humanity, without any written law would suggest, has prescribed that no man shall be called upon to make his defence at a time when his mind is in that situation as not to appear capable of so doing; for, however guilty he may be, the inquiring into his guilt must be postponed to that season, when by collecting together his intellects, and having them entire, he shall be able so to model his defence as to ward off the punishment of the law.

Frith was found insane and "remanded for the present", but like Dyle his fate is unknown. Though Hale suggests that those who were mad on arraignment should be tried on their recovery, it is not clear how often this happened. It was certainly the case, however, for a woman named Milescent who was charged with stealing a petticoat in 1794. Found unfit to be tried, she returned for trial two sessions later when she received what appears to have been a special verdict (the case is recorded in full in Walker, 1968, pp.273–274).

The Criminal Lunatics Act 1800, to be discussed in more detail below (see the section on legislation), saw out the 18th century. Among other things, it stated that in relation to *any* offence, those found insane on arraignment (or later in the trial) should be kept in "strict custody" until His Majesty's Pleasure was known. The Act did not state who should be declared insane or where they should be held, but as will be discussed later, subsequent case law determined that by virtue of the Act all those found unfit for trial, whether because of deafness, mental defect, or insanity, became legally insane. The Act, therefore, formally equated unfitness for trial with insanity, and put into statute what had already been occurring in practice at least in some cases as regards indeterminate detention; it was the penultimate brick in the foundation that would support the modern notion of unfitness to plead.

Thus, between the 14th and 19th centuries, a number of strands were gradually interwoven into a recognisable design. The issues of standing mute, of idiocy, of insanity on arraignment, and of a fair trial were united into a procedure in which a jury was asked to decide two things: First, in the case of muteness, whether failure to plead was intentional or not, and second, regardless of the accused's willingness to enter a plea, whether he or she was mentally defective or insane to the degree that would preclude a fair trial. In the 19th century this design became an established template that would last to the present day.

FRUITION IN THE 19th CENTURY

By the start of the 19th century, all of the elements relevant to the modern notion of unfitness to plead were in place except one: the actual criteria by which an individual was to be found unfit. These criteria emerged in case law through a small number of 19th-century trials, most involving deaf-mutes who were unable to communicate. These "mentally defective" individuals, labelled insane and dealt with under the Criminal Lunatics Act, established a precedent that survived into the 20th century, but which was then applied to those who really did suffer from mental disorder.

The case of Esther Dyson was the first in which the criteria for fitness to plead were clearly enunciated. Dyson, a deaf-mute, was indicted in 1831 for the murder of her bastard child. She was mute in court, and a jury, having heard evidence that she had always been deaf and dumb, found her mute by the visitation of God. An acquaintance then acted as an interpreter, and by making signs Dyson clearly denied the charges. A plea of not guilty was recorded; unfortunately, it was not possible to get her to understand the next, more complex step in the proceedings, her right to challenge jurors. The judge referred to Hale's advice about arraignment during a "phrenzy" (see page 13), and the jury was told that "if they were satisfied that the prisoner had not then, from the defect of her faculties, intelligence enough to understand the nature of the proceedings against her, they ought to find her not sane". The jury was satisfied, and she was therefore found insane and detained under the 1800 Act (R v *Dyson*, 1831).

Perhaps the most important precedent set by *Dyson* was the fact that Bracton's *furiosus* and Hale's *absolutely mad*, both of which would seem to allow for a variety of pathological mental states but which would not obviously include either deafness or idiocy, were replaced by a much more limited concept of insanity related to reason and the ability to understand the nature of court proceedings. More to the point, it brought idiocy under the umbrella of insanity based on what appears to have been a misconstruction of Hale that confounded his comments on idiocy and insanity: In the passage quoted to the jury Hale is referring to the madman in his phrenzy, not to the idiot with no possibility of understanding. For Hale, the idiot and the madman were distinct, and would have required different criteria in relation to determining their fitness for trial. The leap from Dyson's mental deficiency to insanity is thus not a straightforward one, and it is not clear that disposal under the 1800 Act was legally correct (Manson, 1982). But this, of course, was in the days before there was a Court of Appeal, and the misconstruction became further emphasised in the more often quoted case of Pritchard.

Like Dyson, Pritchard was also deaf and dumb. He was indicted for bestiality, but did not plead to the indictment. A jury was empanelled and found Pritchard mute by the visitation of God. It was then asked whether he could plead to the indictment. Pritchard was able to read and write, and on reading the indictment indicated by a sign that he was not guilty. The jury decided that he was in fact *able* to plead. But was he *fit* to plead? The judge went on to ask the jury whether Pritchard was sane or not. Though evidence was given to suggest that he had understood the charge, it was argued that he was "nearly an idiot, and had no proper understanding; and that though he could be made to comprehend some matters, yet he could not understand the proceedings of the trial". Baron Alderson, referring to *Dyson*, went on to give his well-known direction to the jury in which he stated that the question to be decided was whether *"the prisoner has sufficient understanding to comprehend the nature of the trial, so as to make a proper defence to the charge"*.

Alderson said that there were *three* elements that made up a defendant's fitness to stand trial (R v *Pritchard*, 1836, pp.304–305):

> *First*, whether the prisoner is mute of malice or not; *secondly*, whether he can plead to the indictment or not; *thirdly*, whether he is of sufficient intellect to comprehend the course of proceedings on the trial, so as to make a proper defence— to know that he might challenge any of you to whom he may object—and to comprehend the details of the evidence ... It is not enough that he may have a general capacity of communicating on ordinary matters.

Pritchard, based on this direction, was found "not capable of taking his trial", and he was ordered to be confined in prison during His Majesty's Pleasure, replicating the questionable disposal under the 1800 Act that was made in *Dyson*. Even apart from the linking of idiocy with insanity, however, it is not clear that Hale himself would have agreed with the finding, as for him anyone who could read and write was by definition *not* an idiot (Hale, 1971, Vol. i, p.29).

The procedure established by the Pritchard case meant that communication and cognition became clearly defined as the basis for insanity on arraignment, and it became the standard on which decisions about fitness to plead have been made since (though it was in fact concerned with the wider question of fitness to be tried). *First*, an enquiry is made into the cause of muteness, if present, with a finding of mute of malice entailing that fitness to plead is no longer an issue. *Second*, the literal question about a defendant's fitness, or ability, to plead is asked. This relates to the physical capability of communicating a plea, and reflects the fact that the template is based on a model of the deaf-mute defendant. *Finally,* consideration is given to the defendant's cognitive status in relation to his or her ability to comprehend court proceedings, regardless of the defendant's capacity to function in the course of day-to-day affairs.

Thus, three hurdles may need to be jumped before a defendant can be found unfit for trial, related to muteness, fitness to plead, and insanity, though the first and second may be irrelevant, leaving only the last to be negotiated (Prevezer, 1958); indeed, it was over the last hurdle that Pritchard himself fell.

The Pritchard template was further hardened by the case of Berry, a deaf-mute who was found guilty of stealing a watch, a plea of not guilty having been entered by the court on his behalf. Following the verdict, however, the jury was then asked whether Berry was able to understand, and in fact had understood, the proceedings at the trial; it decided that he could not and had not. The case was referred to a higher court, where it was stated that Berry could not be convicted given the jury's secondary finding, and that he should be detained during Her Majesty's Pleasure, even though he was capable of distinguishing right from wrong. The prisoner was not of sane mind because "he has not sufficient *intellect* to understand the nature of the proceedings" (R v *Berry*, 1876, author's italics). It is not clear what would have happened had Berry been found not guilty in the first place.

The demand that the defendant should be capable of instructing legal advisers was a later addition to the criteria that were established in the 1830s.[2] The first clear example in which this requirement was raised was in the case of Davies, an elderly man who along with his son was charged with murder but who stood silent when asked to plead (R v *Davies*, 1853). Here the question was not one of idiocy, but of mental illness. At issue was whether the defendant was incapable of "properly" instructing his counsel because of mental illness. The jury was asked to decide only whether the illness was genuine, with no reference being made to cognitive ability, intelligence, or "sufficient understanding". Indeed, the judge suggested that the jury's decision should be based on the prisoner's appearance and behaviour. On these instructions, the jury decided that Davies' madness was genuine and that he was unfit to plead.

Later rulings have lost sight of the distinction between the mentally defective having sufficient understanding to conduct a defence, and the mentally disordered being sane enough to instruct legal advisers. Instead, the "legal adviser" criterion has been subsumed into those described in *Pritchard*, thereby yoking it, perhaps inappropriately, with cognitive ability. The independent root of the "legal adviser" criterion has been forgotten, and in the process the precedents of *Somervile*, *Dyle*, and *Firth* ignored.

It should also be noted that the criteria established for insanity on arraignment in *Dyson* and *Pritchard* were different to and much wider than those that were set the following decade in the McNaughton Rules in relation to insanity at the time of an offence. In the latter the question to be asked was whether the defendant understood the nature of his or her actions, and if so whether the defendant could recognise them as wrong. But despite the apparently broad sweep of the *Pritchard* decision, unfit to plead findings did not begin to rise to any significant extent until the 1860s. From 1834 to 1866 the rate in nonmurder cases varied from about 30 to 50 per 100,000 persons brought to trial, but from 1866 to 1900 it increased to between 100 and 165 per 100,000 (Walker, 1968). Walker believes that this rise was due to the Prison Act 1865, which required all prisoners to be medically inspected by the prison surgeon. However, the increased availability of legal representation may also have been an important influence. Whatever the cause, the number of individuals found unfit to plead in nonmurder trials continued to rise until it peaked at over 250 per 100,000 trials during the years of the First World War.

20th-CENTURY REFINEMENTS

By the end of the 19th century the concepts of being unfit to plead and unfit to be tried had become largely interchangeable. The meaning of these concepts, and the way in which those found unfit to plead were dealt with by the courts, had assumed its modern form. The core of rational understanding as the definition of unfitness and hence insanity had become solid, and the belief that a trial should not take place in the case of the individual unfit to plead had become unquestioned. This is well illustrated in the case of R v *Governor of H.M. Prison at Stafford, ex p Emery* (1909), in which a deaf and dumb defendant was arraigned for a felony. He was found mute by visitation, and the jury determined that he was incapable of understanding and following the proceedings by reason "of his inability to communicate with and be communicated with by others". Emery's lawyer argued, quite sensibly, that "it would be a straining of language to construe the finding as one of insanity ...", but case law was against him and the judges disagreed, pointing out that "there was no question of general insanity, but only of insanity from the point of view of not understanding the nature of the proceedings". The distorted mould of insanity created in *Dyson* and *Pritchard* had firmly set.

The concept of unfitness to plead, however, and the process to be followed in such cases, did evolve to some extent during the 20th century. Some of the changes were procedural in nature, of practical importance to lawyers but of theoretical interest only to psychiatrists, whereas others were of more direct psychiatric relevance.

The related questions of the point in the proceedings at which the question of fitness to plead should be raised and who could raise it resulted in much judicial disagreement. The issues are important in cases where, though the defendant is clearly unfit to plead, there is doubt about whether he committed the alleged offence. On the one hand, the defence might be reluctant to raise the issue, preferring an acquittal, but the prosecution or judge might feel uneasy in allowing the trial to proceed. In R v *Roberts* (1953), Devlin J. ruled that the case against a deaf-mute accused of murder should be heard even though it was accepted by both sides that there was no means of communicating with him and that he was *de facto* unfit to plead, and despite the prosecution's insistence that the issue of fitness to plead should be determined first. To fail to allow the case to proceed, Devlin said (R v *Roberts,* 1953, p.342):

> ... might result in the grave injustice of detaining as a criminal lunatic a man who was innocent, and, indeed it might result in the public mischief that a person so detained would be assumed ... to have been the person responsible for the crime—whether he was or not—and investigations which might have led to the apprehension of the true criminal would not take place.

This view was echoed, as shall be described, in the thinking behind the Criminal Procedure (Unfitness to Plead and Insanity) Act 1991. However, in *Benyon* the exact opposite position was taken, that is (R v *Benyon*, 1957, p.114):

> ... if the court is aware of the fact that there is a preliminary issue whether the person who is charged before the court on an indictment is insane so that he is unfit to be tried, it is the duty of the court to see that that issue is tried.

The position was finally resolved by statute in the CP(I)A 1964 in which it was stated that the issue, whenever and by whoever raised, could be postponed until the end of the prosecution's case, at which time the charges could be dismissed if the evidence was deficient.

A similar question arises when a defendant insists on pleading guilty in the context of a grossly abnormal mental state, but its resolution is more straightforward (Poole, 1968). In this case, the court is not bound to accept the guilty plea, and can raise the issue of fitness to plead if, as found in R v *Vent* (1935), the accused does not appreciate "the nature of his own confession or the consequences resulting from it". However, it should be noted that this phraseology refers only to the *raising* of the issue, and not to the *determination* of the question itself; Vent's guilty plea to a charge of murder was allowed to stand.

Dispute also emerged over the question of whether it was the defendant who needed to prove fitness (or unfitness) to plead, or whether it was the prosecution that needed to do so (Dean, 1960). For instance, since R v *Turton* (1854) it had been a basic presumption, based on Hale, that a defendant was sane and fit to plead, and it was up to the defence to prove otherwise. In R v *Sharp* (1958), however, it was stated that although it was true that the defendant was presumed fit to plead, if doubts were raised about his or her fitness the defendant should be presumed not to be fit and the onus was then on the prosecution to prove otherwise. The situation was finally settled in R v *Podola* (1959) and R v *Robertson* (1968). In the former case it was confirmed that if the issue was raised by the defence then it was up to the defence to prove, on the balance of probabilities, that the defendant was not fit to plead, and in the latter case it was established that if the issue was raised by the prosecution and contested by the defence, then the prosecution must prove the issue beyond reasonable doubt. No guidance exists, however, of the necessary standard of proof when the issue is raised by the judge.

Although these questions are perhaps of greater legal than psychiatric import, psychiatrists became more involved when 20th-century psychiatric problems tested procedures that were based on 19th-century psychiatric concepts. This was particularly true when the issue was not one of muteness, but of mental disorder. For example, in R v *Robertson* (1968) the defendant, charged with a murder that he readily admitted, suffered from a paranoid illness that made the Crown question his fitness to plead on the grounds that he could not *properly* defend himself: Although Robertson could comprehend court proceedings, a doctor for the Crown said that his "delusional thinking might cause him to act unwisely or otherwise than in his own best interests" (p.557). The defendant himself was unrepresented, and the jury found him unfit to plead. On appeal, however, the Court of Appeal referred to the mentally defective *Pritchard* rather than the mentally ill *Davies*, and the finding of disability was quashed because "the mere fact that the appellant was not capable of doing things which were in his own best interests was insufficient ground for a jury to return a finding of disability" (p.557). In a not dissimilar case involving a man with paranoid schizophrenia who had a "grossly abnormal mental state", the Court of Appeal ruled that "the jury may come to the conclusion that a defendant is highly abnormal, but a high degree of abnormality does not mean that the man is incapable of following a trial or giving evidence or instructing counsel and so on" (R v *Berry*, 1977, p.158).[3] As far as being fit to plead is concerned, paranoid illness is not insanity.

Another attack that the 19th-century structure was able to withstand was related to the notion of memory loss, a test that, perhaps surprisingly, did not occur in English law until it was raised in *Podola* in 1959. Guenther Podola was arrested on charges of blackmail, but escaped by shooting and killing a policeman (Furneaux, 1960). Tracked to his hotel, he was knocked unconscious when the police broke into his room. He claimed that the incident had made him amnesic for the material events of the homicide, and as such he could not instruct his legal advisers so as to make a proper defence; for instance, the killing might have been an accident. The prosecution, however, maintained that the amnesia was not genuine, and after a good deal of medical evidence was presented to the jury by both sides on the nature of "hysterical amnesia", the jury concurred with the prosecution's view. As Podola was not believed, the issue of whether amnesia rendered a defendant unfit to plead was not tested, but because of the importance of the case in relation to another matter,[4] the Home Secretary made a referral to the appellate court. In the course of their opinion, the judges ruled that even if the amnesia had been genuine, Podola would still have been fit to plead because loss of memory did not make one unfit in terms of the *Pritchard* criteria; that is, amnesia does not affect an individual's intellectual capacity to comprehend the nature of the trial. Podola himself was found guilty of murder and executed.

The Butler Committee considered the relevance of amnesia to fitness to stand trial in some detail, and though there was disagreement, the majority view was that amnesia should not make a defendant unfit: "A defendant who is unable to remember the events comprising the alleged offence is really saying that there is another witness, namely himself, who would be able to give an account of what happened but who cannot be put in the witness box because he cannot remember" (Home Office & DHSS, 1975, p.144). The Committee also expressed concern about the difficulty of distinguishing real from feigned memory loss. The minority view was that the situation was not the same as being unable to trace a witness, for there the defendant at least "knows what his defence is and merely cannot produce evidence, whereas the amnesic defendant does not know what his defence might be" (p.145); the majority of the Committee was not swayed by this argument.

Thus, despite its medieval roots and Victorian body, the concept of fitness to plead has withstood the storms of the 20th century, hardly bending but not breaking in the winds of changing psychiatric and legal practice. However, the shape of what we now recognise as fitness to plead has been influenced by more than just legal tradition, case law, and legal precedent; legislation has also had an important influence on it.

LEGISLATION

The *Criminal Lunatics Act*, which was passed in 1800, was part of a trend in both common and statute law whereby attempts were made to prevent dangerous criminal lunatics from menacing the public, though the concern related more to people acquitted because of insanity than to those found insane on arraignment[5] (Manson, 1982). It was enacted following a series of cases in the 18th century involving insane offenders, most immediately Hadfield, for whom the courts had had to resort to *ad hoc* measures in relation to both guilt and sentencing. The Act was intended to regularise the disposal of the insane by the courts and ensure that the dangerous lunatic was not soon set free. It was not concerned with the definition of insanity, leaving this as a question of fact to be decided by jury. Instead, it established a special verdict of not guilty by reason of insanity for the offender who was found to be insane at the time of the offence, and for both the criminally insane and those found insane on arraignment it allowed the Crown to decide where they should be detained, and for how long. The possibility of indeterminate detention for those found unfit to plead thus became sanctioned by legislation. Section 2 of the 1800 Act dealt specifically with the finding of insanity on arraignment (39 & 40 G. 3. c. 93):

> If any person indicted for any offence shall be insane, and shall upon arraignment be found so to be by a jury lawfully impanelled for that purpose, so that such person cannot be tried upon such indictment ... it shall be lawful for the Court ... to direct such finding to be recorded, and thereupon to order such person to be kept in strict custody until His Majesty's Pleasure shall be known; ... in such place and in such manner as to His Majesty shall seem fit.

Once the issue became covered by statute, its position in law remained extremely stable, with no further legislation passed in relation to unfitness to plead for more than 160 years; even then the CP(I)A 1964 merely clarified the position in relation to a number of procedural issues rather than altering the law in any substantial manner. However, the position of those found insane on arraignment was considered on a number of occasions prior to 1964 with no change in law resulting. For instance, the Atkin Committee on Insanity and Crime, meeting in the 1920s with a remit mainly in relation to the insanity defence, also heard evidence concerning unfitness to plead. Its only recommendation regarding unfitness was that evidence from at least two doctors should be required for an unfit to plead finding, but this suggestion was not acted on. The Royal Commission on Capital Punishment, reporting in 1953, made a similar recommendation in relation to the number of doctors who should be involved, but rejected advice that anyone who was insane or mentally defective should on that basis alone be declared unfit for trial.

Other legislation passed between 1800 and 1964, however, did affect, albeit indirectly, the issue of fitness to plead. For instance, the *Prison Act 1865*, mentioned earlier, required all prisoners to be medically examined, increasing the possibility that the issue would at least be considered. Another important influence was the *Homicide Act 1957*, in which the defence of diminished responsibility to a charge of murder meant that being found unfit to plead was no longer one of the few escape routes from the mandatory death penalty of a murder conviction. Between 1900 and 1949, 14% of those committed to trial for murder were found insane on arraignment, but over these years this proportion was not constant; it increased steadily so that over the 10-year period before the Homicide Act was passed, 21% of those committed for trial charged with murder were found unfit on arraignment (Royal Commission on Capital Punishment, 1953; Walker, 1968). The Royal Commission on Capital Punishment believed that this increase reflected a change in attitude among prison medical officers, at least in relation to the death penalty, for whom the test for unfitness became much less stringent than it had been previously.[6] In the eight years after the Homicide Act was passed the proportion of those charged with murder who were found unfit to plead dropped back to 11% (Walker, 1968). The *Mental Health Act 1959*, which provided still more options for dealing with the mentally disordered defendant (such as hospital treatment orders), had perhaps an even greater impact on the need to take the unfit to plead option, with the mean number of findings in relation to those coming to trial decreasing by 40% in the five years after implementation of the Act compared with the five years before it.[7]

Subsequent to the report of the Criminal Law Revision Committee (Home Department, 1963), the *Criminal Procedure (Insanity) Act 1964* was passed. Perhaps reflecting the wording of *Pritchard*, in which the primary question is referred to as fitness to be tried, it refers to any disability in the accused such that ". . . it would constitute a bar to his being tried" rather than to "fitness to plead" *per se*, which appears as a marginal note only; the term "fitness to plead", however, does appear throughout the Committee's report. Sections 4 and 5 of the Act relate to the fitness issue, and deal mainly with procedural matters that had been a source of concern or disagreement by the courts. The Act was not concerned with questions such as how much disability the accused must show before the issue of disability is raised, the degree of proof necessary for the finding, or on whom the burden of proof lies. However, four important points were established by the Act:

- determination of the issue, regardless of who it was raised by, may be postponed until the opening of the case for the defence if it is expedient, and in the interests of the accused, to do so, but no mechanism was provided to allow defence witnesses to be heard;
- following a finding of disability the accused is admitted to a hospital specified by the Secretary of State, to be treated as if he or she were admitted under sections 60 and 65 of the Mental Health Act 1959 (a hospital order with restrictions on discharge unlimited in time);
- if the Secretary of State, after consultation with the responsible medical officer, believes that the accused can be properly tried, then the individual may be remitted to prison to await trial; and
- an accused may appeal against a finding of disability.

In its report the Committee did not recommend any change as to what constitutes unfitness to plead, notwithstanding the problems raised by deaf-mutes and amnesiacs, believing that the decision about what should constitute a bar to trial is best left to the courts. In addition, though it supported the opinion that evidence from two doctors should be required for an unfitness finding, it did not feel that it was necessary to legislate for this as it thought it was already invariably the practice.

Since its passage the CP(I)A 1964 has been criticised on a number of counts. The Butler Committee, for instance, noted with disapproval that the issue could be determined only by a jury in Crown Court and not by magistrates courts, that the *agreed* evidence of two doctors was not mandatory, that there was insufficient provision for a return for trial following recovery, and that the issue of legal representation was not dealt with (Home Office & DHSS, 1975). But the fiercest criticism was reserved for two issues: First, that there was no provision for a so-called trial of the facts to ensure that the accused was in fact responsible for the alleged offence, and second that the court had no option but to impose a hospital order with restrictions on discharge, regardless of whether hospital treatment was necessary or whether the severity of mental disorder was of a degree that would have allowed for compulsory detention and treatment under the Mental Health Act. In relation to this latter point, both Walker (1968) and Poole (1968) made the interesting observation that the CP(I)A had effected a subtle change in relation to disposal in that the 1800 Act allowed the Crown full discretion in deciding the place and manner of custody, but the 1964 Act made it obligatory on the court to impose a hospital order with restrictions.

The strength or otherwise of these criticisms will be discussed in more detail in Chapters 5 and 6. It should be noted, however, that the Report of the Criminal Law Revision Committee (Home Department, 1963) itself reviewed most of these issues. In relation to its failure to provide for a trial of the facts, for example, the Committee's view can be summarised by the statement that "to try a person who has already been found unfit to plead seems to us unacceptable" (p.11). Similarly, when considering the question of disposal, the Committee felt that the Home Office was in a better position than the courts to monitor treatment, and it was concerned that in the absence of restrictions Mental Health Review Tribunals would be able to discharge patients, making the court's detention order ineffective (at that time tribunals did not have the power to discharge restricted patients). Having said this, the Committee did recommend that the court should have the option of an absolute discharge, but this was not incorporated in the Act.

But the heat of the Butler criticisms, together with the publicity generated by a small number of well-publicised cases such as that of Glenn Pearson (Emmins, 1986), and lobbying by the Mental Health Sub-Committee of the Law Society (Law Society, 1991), led, after one or two false starts, to the drafting of a Private Member's Bill that, with Home Office support, became the *Criminal Procedure (Insanity and Unfitness to Plead) Act 1991* (White, 1992). This Act made two important alterations to the law in relation to unfitness to plead: It required the court to conduct a "trial of the facts" after a finding of unfitness to plead in order to determine whether the defendant committed the *actus reus* of the alleged offence, and, with the exception of murder charges, it removed the mandatory hospital and restriction orders, providing the court with four options for disposal: a hospital order (with or without restrictions), a supervision and treatment order, a guardianship order, or an absolute discharge. In addition to these major reforms, the Act also removed the requirement for a return to prison before any subsequent trial could take place, and it finally made statutory the need for evidence from two doctors before the finding can be reached (although the doctors do not need to agree in their evidence).

The 1991 Act, which is the most recent attempt to adapt the notion of unfitness to plead to the 20th century, is not without its critics (White, 1992). The question of whether modest reform can ever shape the concept so that it can fit more easily the contours of the 20th century will be discussed in more detail in Chapter 6.

LEGISLATION IN OTHER COUNTRIES

Though it is beyond the scope of this study to review in any detail the standing of unfitness to plead in other countries, a brief overview of its status internationally is necessary in order to put the English position into perspective and to make sense of much of the research that will be described in the following chapter.

In the developed world, fitness to plead is an issue only in those countries where the criminal justice system is based on the adversarial Anglo-Saxon model. In countries that have an "inquisitorial" style of legal system, as is the case for most of Europe, the concept of fitness to plead does not exist (Harding, 1992). The mental state of the accused is considered only after the facts of the case have been determined, at which point the examining magistrate will request a psychiatric report and, if appropriate, find the defendant "irresponsible" and excuse him from punishment. The question of whether or not the accused could have a fair trial simply does not arise.

In the *United States*, on the other hand, the equivalent issue of competency to stand trial is considered to be of fundamental importance in relation to the mentally disordered defendant, and assessments of competency occur to a much greater extent than they do in England[8] (Pendleton, 1980; Steadman, Monahan, Hartstone, Davis, & Robbins, 1982). Before 1972, a finding of incompetency to stand trial meant, as in England, indefinite detention in hospital. In 1972, however, the Supreme Court ruled that the nature and duration of hospital commitment should relate to the purpose of the committal, and therefore a person committed only on the grounds of incompetency could not be detained for "more than the reasonable period of time necessary to determine whether there is a substantial probability that he will attain that capacity in the foreseeable future" (*Jackson* v *Indiana,* 1972, p.738). The various states have interpreted this ruling in different ways, with some allowing the court to decide what is a reasonable time in individual cases, others setting time limits dependent on the alleged crime, and still others simply setting maximum time limits (Golding & Roesch, 1988). The test for competency itself was established in *Dusky* v *United States* (1960), and requires the defendant to have "sufficient present ability to consult with his lawyer with a reasonable degree of rational understanding and [to have] a rational as well as a factual understanding of the proceedings against him". This has since been modified by statute in the Comprehensive Crime Control Act 1984 so that the defendant must be "presently suffering from a mental disease or defect rendering him mentally incompetent to the extent that he is unable to understand the nature and consequences of the proceedings against him or to assist properly in his defence" (Harding, 1992). Thus, the United States differs from England not only in its greater concern about the issue of competency, but also in defining competency through legislation; however, the United States is similar in linking the concept with rationality and understanding.

In *Canada*, the legal position was amended in 1992. The criteria for being found unfit to plead are now specified in the federal criminal code: An individual must be unable to understand the nature of court proceedings and possible outcomes, or be unable to communicate with counsel. The Crown must demonstrate that there is a case to answer. Once found unfit, disposals include absolute or conditional discharges, and limited or indefinite hospital treatment orders. Those detained in hospital as unfit are subject to the oversight of a review board, which has now been given the power to order the transfer or discharge of the patient (Harding, 1992).

Like Canada, most *Australian* states follow the English model of transfer to hospital with restrictions on discharge following an unfitness finding. In New South Wales, however, the law was reformed in 1983 so that after the finding a decision is made by a Mental Health Review Tribunal about whether fitness is likely to be regained within a year; if not, what amounts to a "trial of the facts" takes place. If a "qualitative finding of guilt" is reached, a period is fixed beyond which detention in either prison or hospital is not allowed. This period of detention can be no longer than that which would have followed an actual guilty verdict; if the tribunal does not consider the person to be dangerous, however, then release must be recommended within a year (Harding, 1992; MacFarlane, 1987).

The legal position in *Scotland* in relation to the equivalent "insanity in bar of trial" also differs in important ways from the situation in England. The authority to find an individual unfit to stand trial is more widely available in Scotland, and the issue can be determined not only in the High Court, but also in Sheriff Courts, which have some summary jurisdiction (Scottish Home and Health Department and Crown Office, 1975). Consequently, unfitness findings occur with much greater frequency than they do south of the border. In addition, though orders restricting discharge are required in relation to solemn (indictment) proceedings, in summary proceedings they are not mandatory and are infrequently imposed (Normand, 1984). The criteria for determining insanity in bar of trial, however, are similar to those in England

(Chiswick, 1978; Poole, 1968), and as in England before the law was reformed in 1991, there is no mechanism for a trial of facts. Also as in England, a committee (the Thomson Committee) was set up to review criminal procedure; it reported in 1975 and made a number of recommendations for reform in relation to fitness to plead[9] (Scottish Home and Health Department and Crown Office, 1975). Again, as in England, none of the recommendations were implemented (Normand, 1984).

Thus, although the concept of fitness to plead is broadly similar in all the countries reviewed, the procedures involved and the implications of the finding differ, with a variety of combinations. However, in no country is the issue free of controversy, and in all criticism of current practice and proposals for reform seem to be as common as they are in England (Golding & Roesch, 1988).

CONCLUSION

This chapter has reviewed the historical development of the concept of fitness to plead and the procedures that have evolved to deal with those considered to be unfit for trial. The 20th-century concept is still very much what it was in the 19th century, though new rationales have been put forward for its maintenance, ranging from ensuring that court proceedings are accurate, to protecting the dignity of the court, to maximising the efficacy of punishment by making certain that the accused appreciates the wrongness of what he or she has done (Verdun-Jones, 1981). Only recently have the consequences of the finding become less severe in England and Wales.

Though a historical review of this type can make sense of the tradition, case law, and legislation that make up the theory of what it means to be unfit to plead, the effect that the finding actually has on those who come within its orbit can be determined only by studying the procedure in practice. The next chapter, therefore, reviews the research that has been carried out in relation to those found unfit to plead to criminal charges.

NOTES

1. Hale followed Coke's earlier classification of the *non compos mentis* as idiots, lunatics, distracted persons, and drunkards.
2. Indeed, access to counsel was not routine in the early part of the 19th century, being restricted to only the most serious of offences.

3. It is perhaps ironic that this case, which involved a man named Berry, made a distinction between schizophrenia and insanity, whereas exactly 100 years earlier another case, also involving a man named Berry, established that idiocy *was* a form of insanity.

4. The question of the burden of proof; amnesia was in fact only a secondary issue.

5. Walker quotes the Attorney-General's introduction of the Act to the House of Commons: "It has been found that persons who have done the most shocking acts, and who have been acquitted on the grounds of being deranged in their intellects, having been allowed to go at large have afterwards committed similar acts again" (Walker, 1963, p.43).

6. The Commission said that they had been told by the prison medical officers that "unfitness to plead means insanity in the ordinary medical sense" (p.77). It is likely, however, that this was true only in murder cases, otherwise it is hard to make sense of the Commission's later comment that "The general view ... was that someone who is certifiably insane may often nevertheless be fit to plead to the indictment ... [and] if he is, he should ordinarily be allowed to do so" (p.78).

7. Figures from HMSO: *Criminal Statistics for England and Wales.* From 1956 to 1960, the mean number of unfitness findings per 100,000 trials was 200.0 a year (SD 29.8), whereas from 1961 (the first full year that the MHA 1959 was in effect) to 1965 the mean was 122.2 (SD 8.0), a statistically significant drop ($t = 5.64$, $df = 8$, $P < 0.001$); the difference in terms of actual number of cases was also significantly less in the five years after the Act, declining from an average of 51.7 (SD 6.4) cases per year from 1956 to 1960 to an average of 36 (SD 7.1) from 1961 to 1965 ($t = 3.67$, $df = 8$, $P < 0.01$).

8. In the 1970s it was estimated that more than half of all criminal commitments to hospital were on the grounds of incompetency to stand trial (Pendleton, 1980).

9. It is interesting that unlike the Butler Committee, the Thomson Committee did prefer the terminology "unfitness to plead". Also, unlike most commentators south of the border, it felt that unfitness should be firmly defined and statutory, with the test being "Is the accused incapable by reason of mental disorder (including deficiency) of understanding the substance of the charge and proceedings and of communicating adequately with his legal advisers" (Scottish Home and Health Department and Crown Office, 1975, p.214).

CHAPTER THREE

Review of the research literature

A number of assumptions are often made about individuals who are found unfit to plead in England and Wales, and about what happens to them. For instance, it has been said that the unfit to plead tend to suffer from serious mental disorder, that they usually have been charged with severe offences, that the cases against them are almost always clear-cut, that they are rarely remitted back for trial, and that they are detained for longer periods, in hospitals with more secure conditions, then would otherwise be the case (Chiswick, 1990a; Gostin, 1986; Home Office & DHSS, 1975; Royal Commission on Capital Punishment, 1953; Walker, 1968). However, these assertions are on the whole dependent on expert testimony and clinical impression, much of which is now dated. As mentioned in Chapter 1, before some of the findings contained in this report were published (Grubin, 1991a,b,c), research accounts relating to unfitness to plead in England and Wales barely existed.

The research situation in North America is somewhat different. There, studies have focused on a variety of issues relating to those found incompetent to stand trial, ranging from the characteristics of incompetent defendants, to medium- and long-term outcome, to the assessment of competency itself. The greater emphasis that is placed on the evaluation of competency in both the United States and Canada, however, means that the problems encountered there are to some extent different from those found in the UK, and not all of the research will be relevant to a UK setting. The resonances, however, are often similar enough to harmonise with the situation in the UK, and it will be seen that some of the results of the American work provide suggestions of what may also be the case in the UK; American findings may in addition hold clues about the ways in which recent reforms in England may affect English defendants who are unfit to plead.

ENGLAND AND WALES

In comparison with what has actually been published, more but a still limited amount of research appears to have taken place over the years for the various committees that have looked into the issue of fitness to plead, with results surfacing as occasional statements of fact within larger formal reports. For instance, the Report of the Criminal Law Revision Committee (Home Department, 1963, p.9) was able to say that "There seems to be a general impression that the accused is always sent to Broadmoor and detained there for a long time. But in fact the numbers of persons so found who are detained there or in one of the other special hospitals (Rampton and Moss Side) and of those detained in local hospitals are nearly equal; transfers from special to local hospitals are frequent and discharges are not infrequent". In a similar way, the Butler Committee (p.147) was told by the Home Office that "the Home Secretary's power to remit the accused person for trial is sparingly used …". Unfortunately, without the relevant data it is difficult to know what "sparingly used" means in practice, how many patients are in fact transferred out of special hospital, or the number of patients unfit to plead who are in the end discharged from hospital.

A large number of case reports relating to individuals found unfit to plead have also been published, mostly in the form of trial accounts similar to those described in Chapter 2. Written from a legal perspective, not surprisingly they contain only a limited amount of information about mental state, diagnosis, and similar items of psychiatric interest. Even from the legal point of view, however, these cases cannot be taken as representative; indeed, one of the reasons such cases are reported in the first place is because of their special interest. This is perhaps well illustrated by the full history of the Glenn Pearson case given by Emmins (1986). Glenn Pearson was mentally handicapped and suffered from pre-lingual deafness (deaf-mutism). He was charged in 1983 with stealing £5 and three light bulbs from a neighbour's house. He was able to communicate and understand only very simple concepts, and he was found unfit to plead when he appeared in court. Following the finding he was transferred from prison to a local hospital for the mentally handicapped, and three months later he was discharged by a Mental

Health Review Tribunal, with the police simply allowing the charges to lapse. Emmin's main concern was that a trivial offence could have had potentially drastic consequences for Pearson, given the necessary imposition of a restriction order and given that he would never become fit for trial. However, if one subscribes to the general assumptions that the unfit to plead have committed serious crimes and that they are detained for long periods in secure hospitals, then the Glenn Pearson case must be the exception rather than the rule.

The three case histories described by Wood and Guly (1991), written from a psychiatric perspective and which do in fact contain much psychiatric detail, again illustrate that caution must be used in generalising from case reports. All three of their cases involved individuals who were charged with murder. Two of the accused were mentally handicapped, and the evidence against them consisted primarily of their own inconsistent and periodically retracted confessions; in one of these cases the real murderer was eventually arrested and convicted, but the mentally handicapped defendant (who also had a concomitant psychotic illness) had by then spent over a year in hospital as unfit to plead. The authors' intention was to highlight a number of issues relating to unfitness to plead, including the problems of confessions in the mentally disordered, the difficulties of obtaining pre-trial hospital assessments in cases of murder, and the potential advantages to be gained by having a "trial of the facts" after an unfit to plead finding. Wood and Guly made no claims about the representative nature of their cases, and there is no way of knowing how often the issues they raise occur. Indeed, based on case reports, one might assume that the mentally handicapped made up a majority of those found unfit to plead.

The one piece of English research that does appear in the pre-1991 psychiatric literature provides little additional light on the psychiatric aspects of unfitness to plead (Larkin & Collins, 1989). This was a retrospective study that analysed 77 psychiatric reports prepared at the time of trial for 31 individuals held in Rampton special hospital as unfit to plead. The authors found that the issue was actually mentioned in less than two-thirds of the reports (62%), and in those reports that did comment on fitness 37% contained only what the authors called nonstandard criteria (that is, factors relating to neither the *Pritchard* criteria nor those recommended by the Butler Committee). However, given that psychiatric evidence in relation to fitness to plead is usually given orally in court and led by a barrister, the Larkin and Collins study may reflect more a poor standard of report writing than psychiatric confusion *per se*; in addition, of course, the mental state of many of the patients may have changed between the time the reports were written and the time of the trial. But it should also be remembered that the actual decision of whether a defendant is unfit to plead is made by a jury following direction by a judge, and not by the psychiatrist. The study would have been of greater value if it had contained more detail about the patients, in particular about their mental states at the time of trial, diagnoses, and mental states while in Rampton, but even then its exclusive special-hospital population would have made it impossible to generalise from the findings.

Before concluding this section on research that has taken place in England and Wales, the paucity of which cannot be overemphasised, it is worth mentioning a study by Mackay (1991) that appeared at about the same time as did the three papers containing some of the research described in more detail here (Grubin, 1991a,b,c). Mackay's study was based on the same Home Office files as the research reported here, though it covered a slightly different time span, 1979–1989 compared with 1976–1988. From a lawyer's point of view this study includes more information then is normally found in legal case reports, but it provides a somewhat superficial account of the data and from a psychiatric perspective it is of limited use. For instance, the percentage of individuals with previous convictions is given, but there is no breakdown of what these were for or how serious the offences were; it is also said that over 80% of the population had "some form of psychiatric history" but no further comment is made about these histories. This type of information does not show, for example, whether the population is composed of individuals who are primarily mentally disordered and who have had isolated police contact, whether it is one of habitual offenders who have only minor mental disorder, or whether it is in fact similar to the normal range of mentally disordered offenders who come before the courts every day. The curious assertion was also made that despite only four reports mentioning all of the standard criteria, "it seemed to be accepted by all concerned that the criteria in question are individually necessary and individually sufficient conditions for a finding of disability". This is simply wrong because if all the criteria were in fact necessary then there could only have been four unfitness to plead findings over the years that Mackay surveyed.

It should also be noted that the Mackay paper was inaccurate in respect of the number of individuals who were found unfit to plead each year. This error arose because cases that were referred to in documentation but not officially recorded were not followed up.

Mackay concludes that his findings support the proposal for a trial of the facts that was being put forward by the Law Society at the time. This was based primarily on the fact that there were eight cases in which individuals were acquitted on return for trial. However, as will be described later (see p. 78), the majority of these acquittals were technical in nature, arising either because the prosecution saw no purpose in pursuing the case further, or because the prosecution's case became weaker with the passage of time. In any case, the issues surrounding a trial of facts are in fact quite complex (see also Chapter 6). Because defendants who were found unfit to plead are later acquitted does not mean that they would have benefited from a trial of the facts; indeed, without their active participation such a trial might have found them guilty when, given time to recover, a full trial could potentially find them not guilty.

SCOTLAND

In Scotland, where there are proportionally many more cases of the equivalent finding of insanity in bar of trial then there are in England, the situation has been researched to a slightly better extent. Chiswick (1978) was able to review the notes of all 65 patients detained as insane in bar of trial in Carstairs, the special hospital for Scotland, as of October 1976. He compared these patients with a control group who had been admitted to the hospital for other reasons. He found that those detained as insane in bar of trial were slightly older at the time of their court appearances, had significantly less previous criminal behaviour (with a third having no criminal record), were more likely to have been charged with homicidal crimes (50% of them), and were more likely to have a diagnoses of psychotic illness (personality disorder and mental subnormality were more common in the control group). He also found that they had been detained for a significantly longer period of time in Carstairs, with an average admission length of over 11 years compared with about 7 years for the control group.

Though not representative of all those found unfit to plead in Scotland, the Chiswick study would have included most of the more serious offences as the majority of those found insane in bar of trial to an indictable offence are sent to the state hospital, as are those who are accused of serious summary offences (Normand, 1984). The diagnostic differences between the groups found by Chiswick are perhaps what one would have predicted, particularly as personality disorder, other than in exceptional cases, would not usually be expected to produce a mental state that would lead to an insanity in bar of trial finding. However, the lower incidence of previous criminal behaviour is notable, suggesting that there may be a subgroup among those found insane in bar of trial who differ in important respects from more typical mentally disordered offenders found in special hospital, where previous convictions are common (as they were in Chiswick's control group). Also of interest was the longer length of stay among those found insane in bar of trial. There was not enough information to determine the cause of this, but Chiswick suggests that it may reflect either illnesses that are more severe in the insane in bar of trial population, or the more serious nature of their offences (50% had been charged with homicide); if the latter is the case, however, it should not be forgotten that these are individuals who have not actually been tried and convicted.

The issue of remission for trial in Scotland in cases where fitness is recovered has been looked at in detail by Normand (1984). He points out that information about recovery of fitness and reprosecution in Scotland is difficult to obtain, but as far as he could ascertain from enquiries made to the Crown Office and Procurator Fiscal Service this has occurred only in a small number of cases, mainly involving serious offences where fitness to plead was regained in a short period of time. Normand surveyed all cases of individuals admitted to Carstairs as insane in bar of trial between 1978 and 1983, as well as all cases of insane in bar of trial to charges of murder between 1973 and 1983. Of the 10 patients accused of murder, 2 were subsequently tried,[1] whereas in none of the 25 nonmurder cases were proceedings resumed.[2] Normand discovered one other case, not involving a Carstairs patient, of an individual charged with fraud who had been committed to a local hospital; it emerged that he had feigned mental illness and proceedings were resumed. Chiswick (1990b) describes two other cases, again involving rapid recovery, in which patients were returned for trial; in both cases the accompanying procedural confusion was great.

The small number of individuals found insane in bar of trial in Scotland who are eventually returned to court is notable. The feeling appeared to be that where a post-conviction hospital order was likely there was little point in remitting for trial. This is a somewhat illogical position because if guilt is so clear then there would seem to be little point in going through the motions of an insane in bar of trial hearing; instead, it would be more straightforward to convict with a definitive disposal. These points will be discussed further in Chapter 6.

NORTH AMERICA

As described earlier, in England there has been little information available until recently about what happens to individuals after they have been found unfit to plead. In the United States, however, a number of researchers have investigated outcome for those found incompetent to stand trial, both before and after indeterminate detention was declared unconstitutional in *Jackson* v *Indiana* (1972). Prior to this important ruling, a number of investigators had noted that many patients who had been found incompetent to stand trial never left hospital. For instance, in a Michigan state hospital where 705 out of 1484 patients were detained as incompetent, a survey estimated that more than 50% of the incompetent patients would never be released (Hess & Thomas, 1963), though the study itself was notable for its almost complete lack of data. A somewhat better report from a high-security Massachusetts hospital noted that before 1960 "more of this type of patient had left [the hospital] by dying than by all other avenues combined" (McGarry, 1971).

Both the Michigan and the Massachusetts studies commented on the fact that once found incompetent to stand trial and committed to hospital, the judicial system seemed to lose interest in the patient, and the medical system in the issue. In the McGarry study, for example, the author and his colleagues interviewed all those who were detained as incompetent at the end of 1963. It was found that 56 of 189 (30%) had regained their competency, and through the intervention of the author they were returned to court for trial. The median length of hospital detention for these patients was two years, but three men had been detained for over 15 years. McGarry went on to follow up these and another 15 patients who were brought back for trial. Of the 71 men, the charges against 24 (34%) were dropped on return to court (including those against 11 of the 12 men charged with misdemeanours), 14 (20%) received prison sentences, 14 (20%) were found not guilty by reason of insanity and returned to the hospital, and the remainder seem to have received some sort of community disposal; there do not appear to have been any not guilty findings. By 1969, five years after they had been tried, 50 (70%) had "reached the community"; half were subsequently rehospitalised or imprisoned "usually for brief periods", and about the same number were accused of further crimes. We do not know, of course, what would have happened to the majority of these patients had they not been subsumed into the study, but McGarry observed that of 191.9 years of potential freedom for the 50 men, 159.3 years were realised.

There are few recent data available in relation to the duration of hospital commitment or the type of treatment those found incompetent receive, but the fate of those found incompetent to stand trial in the United States appears to have improved since the 1972 *Jackson* ruling, at least in terms of the length of time they are detained in hospital as incompetent. In 1978, for instance, a national survey found that 32% of all mentally disordered offenders admitted to hospital were detained on the grounds of incompetency to stand trial, with an average length of stay of approximately six months (Steadman et al., 1982). The effect of the *Jackson* decision is well illustrated by two more localised studies. In Los Angeles, a random sample of all those found incompetent to stand trial in 1983 was followed up for two years (Lamb, 1987). At the end of the follow-up period, only 2 of 85 individuals remained in hospital as incompetent to stand trial, with 84% having regained their competency (in a median time of 10 months) and 42% released without trial. A Michigan study involving all those found incompetent to stand trial in the state over a two-year period ($N = 222$) reported that 90% regained their competency and were returned to court within 15 months (Mowbray, 1979). In both of these studies, as in the Massachusetts study described earlier, it was of interest that though charges were frequently dropped when defendants were returned to court, acquittals were extremely rare.

The sharp reduction in the length of hospital detention that has occurred subsequent to the *Jackson* decision in the United States is worth noting in view of the fact that the legal situation in the United States pre-*Jackson* resembled that of England prior to 1992 and the reform of the law in relation to unfitness to plead.

But who is being found incompetent to stand trial in the United States? Perhaps surprisingly this question has been looked at in very few studies. The Los Angeles work suggests that those who are incompetent to stand trial are predominantly psychotic males in their thirties who have both criminal and psychiatric histories and who often come from ethnic minorities (Lamb, 1987). In that study, the mean age of those found incompetent was 30 (range 18–67), just 32% were white (though no comparison figures are given in relation to the catchment area population), 84% suffered from schizophrenia, another 7% from a major affective disorder, and just 1% were diagnosed as having severe mental retardation and 1% as having an antisocial personality disorder; 86% had been psychiatric in-patients in the past, more than 20% were of no fixed abode, and only 8% had no criminal record. About half the sample were what Lamb described as "psychotic sporadic offenders", that is, individuals with a history of severe mental illness but with little serious previous criminal history, but 70% of this sporadic minor offender group were now held on charges relating to serious violence. It was Lamb's view that these were individuals for whom neither criminal justice nor mental health systems were willing to take responsibility, and findings of incompetency were just one way in which they were juggled between the two.

Other American research tends to support the general profile found in the Los Angeles study, though comparisons are difficult because similar categories are not always used and precise figures are often not given. A description of individuals found incompetent to plead to misdemeanour charges in New York, for instance, found that whites were underrepresented, that nearly two-thirds had schizophrenia, and that previous hospitalisation was common (Rachlin, Stokman, & Grossman, 1986); in Michigan only about a third of those found incompetent in the mid-1970s were white (Mowbray, 1979); in Alaska 60% had schizophrenia (Phillips, Wolf, & Coons, 1988); in both North Carolina in the early 1970s (Roesch, 1979) and in Virginia between 1985 and 1987 (Warren, Fitch, Dietz, & Rosenfeld, 1991) mentally retarded individuals made up nearly a fifth of those found incompetent to stand trial.

Some North American writers have argued that incompetency is used as a way of bypassing legal barriers to civil commitment, so that the nondangerous mentally ill individual who would otherwise have been released by the courts can still be detained; in other words, it is a means of controlling social deviance (Geller & Lister, 1978; Verdun-Jones, 1981). Perhaps the most vocal proponent of this view is Szasz (1968), who also suggested that incompetency can act as an effective means of denying those with dissident views access to the courts. He cites Ezra Pound as a classic example. Pound, found incompetent to stand trial on charges of treason, was detained in a psychiatric hospital for 13 years, but when finally released the charges against him were dropped. Further support for the view that incompetency may be a way of controlling social deviance comes from Wisconsin, where, after civil commitment statutes became more restrictive, the number of civil commitments declined whereas the number of competency evaluations increased by up to 200% (Dickey, 1980; Treffert, 1979; both quoted in Miller & Germain, 1987).

What evidence there is, however, does not support the assertion that incompetency is used to detain individuals within the mental health system who otherwise would have slipped through the criminal justice net. Most studies have found that only a small minority of those found incompetent to stand trial in the United States were charged with minor offences, and despite the rise in the number of those found incompetent to stand trial that has accompanied the tightening up of civil commitment laws, the proportion of those found incompetent in relation to minor charges has not risen (Arvanites, 1989; Lamb, 1987).

Those who are actually found to be incompetent to stand trial in the United States, however, are only a minority of those whose competency is evaluated. The assessment of competency, which is often cursory in the UK, is emphasised to a great extent in the United States. Steadman et al. (1982), for instance, estimated that there are 3–4 admissions to hospital for an *evaluation* of competency for every positive finding. The ratio of positive findings, however, may actually be much less: In a

Massachusetts study, for example, only 2 of 87 cases resulted in an incompetency decision[3] (Geller & Lister, 1978); in a study in Alaska 10% of 1063 evaluations made over a five-year period produced an incompetency recommendation (Phillips et al., 1988); in Mississippi 11% of 232 referrals over two years were found incompetent (Nicholson & Johnson, 1991); and in Virginia 17% of 773 referrals over two years were judged to be incompetent (Warren et al., 1991).

The cost of in-patient competency evaluations is high in comparison with the number of positive findings they produce, but in any case the motivation behind many evaluations has been questioned as not relating to true concern about the possibility of a fair trial. Cooke, Johnston, and Pogany (1973), for example, found that referrals for evaluation in Michigan reflected proximity to urban areas and the seriousness of the offence, with 12% of individuals charged with homicide undergoing competency evaluations, and suggested that more sophisticated city lawyers may use competency evaluations as a way of preparing for an eventual insanity defence. Warren et al. (1991) argued that evaluations may also be a way of gaining information with which to plea bargain or to encourage leniency in sentencing, or as a way for lawyers to ensure "that they have adequately represented their client rather than foreclosing a psychiatric defence without the benefit of expert consultation". Rappeport, Conti, and Rudnick (1983) were more blunt, claiming that the majority of competency evaluations were unnecessary, and that on occasions they may simply be used to delay trials that fall at inconvenient times. But evaluations may also be used by lawyers for the perhaps more laudable, though still camouflaged, aim of obtaining treatment for a defendant who can not be committed under civil law[4]. Because of the possible misuse of competency evaluations, a number of states have now initiated programmes designed to screen out inappropriate competency referrals: The programme in Maryland described by Rappeport et al. (1983) allowed only about one in three referrals to proceed to an assessment in hospital in 1982, saving the state more than $450,000.

Research in Canada has produced similar results to that in the United States. Thus, evaluations are not uncommon but findings of unfitness are infrequent: 3% of all pre-trial referrals over 10 years at a Saskatchewan hospital where 75% of such examinations in the province took place (Kunjukrishnan, 1979), and in a study of six large cities 15% of all referrals (Menzies, Webster, Butler, & Turner, 1980). In terms of their characteristics, a study in British Columbia of 106 unfit to plead defendants who regained their capacity to plead between 1977 and 1979 found that two-thirds had past psychiatric histories, 90% were psychotic, and about half were either transient or living in a hostel at the time of arrest. However, more than half, a much higher proportion than is usually found in the US studies, were charged with less serious, nonviolent offences[5] (Roesch, Eaves, Sollner, Normendin, & Glackman, 1981), but this may simply be a reflection of the fact that all those in the study had been discharged and hence may have represented the less serious end of the offence spectrum; it has been found in the United States, for instance, that length of detention is correlated with the seriousness of the charge (Cuneo, Brelje, Randolph, & Taliana, 1982).

Information about the duration of commitment following an unfit finding is even more difficult to obtain in Canada then it is in the United States as most studies have looked at all those held on warrants of the Lieutenant Governor, a mixed group of individuals found unfit for trial, not guilty by reason of insanity, and transferred from prison. A national survey in 1974 found that for this whole group, mean periods of hospital detention ranged from 56 months in Quebec to 134 months in Manitoba, with a national mean of 69 months, but the authors did comment that the unfit to plead were held in custody for longer periods (Quinsey & Boyd, 1977, quoted in Verdun-Jones, 1981). It is interesting, however, that in the 1974 survey, 43% of those held on warrants were unfit to plead, but in 1983 the proportion had dropped to 14% (Webster et al., 1985, quoted in Mackay, 1990). This fall seems to have been due to an increased turnover of the unfit to plead. In Ontario, for instance, of the 103 warrants issued in the year from 1st March, 1988, 67% were in relation to unfitness, but only 8% of all those held on warrants were unfit for trial: 60% of the "vacated" warrants related to individuals who had been found unfit to plead (Zellerer, 1989, quoted in Mackay, 1990).

Further information about length of detention in Canada comes from the British Columbia study referred to earlier (Roesch et al., 1981). There it was found that the mean length of detention for those who had been discharged was 173 days, with a median of 139 days, though this of course says little about length of stay for those who have not been released. But this type of finding, taken together with the evidence of increased turnover of those held on warrants as unfit, suggests that the length of detention for those held as unfit to plead in Canada may have dropped in a way similar to, though perhaps not as substantially as, the United States, even without the stimulus of a *Jackson*-type decision. It may be the case that practice in Canada has been strongly influenced by events in the United States.

THE ASSESSMENT OF COMPETENCY
IN NORTH AMERICA

In view of the frequency with which competency evaluations take place in North America, it is perhaps not surprising that a good deal of research effort has been put into analysing how psychiatrists reach decisions about competency to stand trial. Early workers were not impressed with what they found. Hess and Thomas (1963), for instance, claimed that psychiatric practice was often confused, and in any case seemed to consist "of simply parroting the language of the statute with the insertion of the appropriate negative or positive words" (p.715). Furthermore, though reliability between different interviewers is usually found to be good, normally above 80% (Golding, Roesch, & Schreiber, 1984; Phillips et al., 1988), it has been pointed out that because most of those who are assessed are in fact competent, this high rate actually reflects agreement about who is *competent* to stand trial rather than about those who are incompetent (Golding et al., 1984).

In an attempt to make the concept of competency more objective, specific checklists and operational criteria have been advocated, though the various instruments have been evaluated to only a limited extent (Golding & Roesch, 1988; McGarry, 1973, quoted in Schreiber, 1982; Robey, 1965). On the whole, however, these tests have sought validity by comparing their results with those of actual competency decisions, a circular approach that assumes that "competency" is an objective entity that psychiatrists are accurately diagnosing and that the instruments can match. Other workers have attempted to define criteria for competency through MMPI results, again relying on actual decisions of psychiatrists to establish validity (Maxson & Neuringer, 1970).

More recently, Roesch and his colleagues have sought to develop an instrument that would leave the construct of competency open rather than defining it rigidly, the specifics being a matter for personal judgement (Golding & Roesch, 1988; Roesch et al., 1984; Schreiber, Roesch, & Golding, 1987). Their approach concentrates on providing a structured assessment interview that ensures a consistent collection of data relating to both legal functioning and mental state. The reliability of their "Interdisciplinary Fitness Interview" (IFI) is said to be good, with a study of pre-trial assessments in Boston producing overall agreement in 97% of cases (Golding et al., 1984). It is interesting, however, that correspondence with staff from the hospital who were carrying out the actual assessments for the court was poor, with 76% overall agreement but agreement specifically about incompetency of just 58%. It may be that the IFI allowed the researchers to think more clearly about the competency issue, but it may also be the case that competency means different things to different people. The question of what competency is, therefore, remains an open one. It must be added, however, that most researchers working in the area do not believe that lengthy and expensive institutional evaluations can provide any better answer to this question than can a single out-patient interview.

Though the definition of incompetency remains unclear, the belief that it can be assessed objectively remains a feature of American writing about the topic. Associated with this notion is the belief that incompetency is also something that can, and should, be treated. Indeed, because the *Jackson* decision requires that hospital commitment should relate to the nature and purpose of the committal, some have argued that it is wrong for forensic facilities to place more emphasis on "treating mental disability than on the specific symptoms that legally define incompetence to stand trial" (Siegel & Elwork, 1990, p. 57), a concept that might seem strange to psychiatrists in Britain. Regardless, a survey in the United States found that in 43% of the clinics that responded to the request for information, the treatment of patients who were incompetent to stand trial was in fact different from that of other patients, with a concentration on the restoration of competency at the expense of other factors (Siegel & Elwork, 1990).

A number of treatment programmes directed specifically at improving competency have been reported in the literature, and a high efficacy has been claimed for them. A programme in California, for instance, was designed "to eliminate or reduce those symptoms that interfere with standing trial", and involved competency classes and mock trials; a 90% success rate was reported (Pendleton, 1980). These competency treatment programmes, however, have not on the whole been tested in controlled studies. An exception was a study in Philadelphia in which incompetent defendants were divided into treatment and control groups, with the treatment group receiving instruction in court functioning (Siegel & Elwork, 1990). Improvement in competency was greater in the treatment group, with 43% judged by hospital staff to have regained their competency compared with 15% of the control group. Unfortunately, it was not clear from the report whether these judgements were made blind to the treatment conditions, nor was information provided about general improvement of or deterioration in mental state, or indeed information about whether the patients were predominantly psychotic or mentally handicapped. Nevertheless, one must wonder whether incompetency can really be isolated into as pure a culture as these workers seem to suggest, and if it can, whether psychiatrists should be directing their energies towards educating patients about court procedure in preference to treating mental disorder.

CONCLUSION

Research from both the United Kingdom and North America has provided a partial profile of individuals who are found unfit to plead, though the question of whether or not they differ in important ways from the vast number of mentally disordered defendants who appear before the courts annually remains unanswered; given the prevalence of psychiatric and criminal features in their backgrounds, the suggestion would be that they do not. What is clear is that whereas much of the law in relation to the unfit to plead developed in the context of mentally handicapped defendants, the process is now much more relevant to those who are psychotic. This has created curious distortions not only in the legal framework, but also in psychiatric practice as the psychiatrist must juggle with different, sometimes conflicting concepts of insanity. This may reflect the ritualistic origins of the notion of unfitness to plead described in Chapter 2.

As the guise of ensuring a fair trial being the primary motivating factor for finding an individual unfit to plead has worn thin, the essential question has become whether being found unfit to plead works in the interest of the mentally disordered defendant, either in terms of legal outcome or psychiatric treatment. The research from North America suggests that there the answer to the former question is yes, in that in the proper hands it can be a useful part of the lawyer's armoury. The answer to the latter question, however, would seem to be no, in that being found unfit to plead appears to have become a component of the community-prison-court-hospital-community cycle. Whether or not this is also true in England is one question the present research sets out to answer.

NOTES

1.   In both of the murder cases that returned for trial, psychiatrists at the state hospital who examined the patients soon after admission disagreed that they were unfit for trial, and in each case the patient was reassessed and returned to court within months; both received prison sentences.
2.   Though none of the nonmurder cases returned for trial, resumption of proceedings was considered in two cases in which recovery had been relatively rapid. In one the Crown decided to restart proceedings, but the patient had in the meantime been discharged, readmitted to a local hospital, and discharged again to out-patient care. The Procurator Fiscal did not learn of the second discharge for some months, by which time the patient was stable and in work, and in the end criminal proceedings were not resumed. The other case involved an offence against an 11-year-old

girl, and though the Crown intended to bring the case back for trial, it did not do so because of "evidential considerations" and concern for the victim.

3. Some of the 87 cases may have involved admission for other reasons, however.

4. Writers like Szasz, of course, would not praise this type of attempt to gain treatment for a mentally disordered offender, and would instead condemn the practice as simply labelling offenders as insane and confining them to hospital without the benefit of a trial.

5. As Cooke et al. (1973) point out, however, there are many more arrests for less serious offences. Thus, if the number of findings is viewed as a function of arrest rates for specific crimes, then unfitness findings per offence type become proportionally much greater for more serious offences.

CHAPTER FOUR

Methodology

C3 is the division of the Home Office that has responsibility for mentally disordered offenders. In particular, it oversees the management of all patients who have had restrictions placed on their discharge by the courts under the provisions of section 41 of the Mental Health Act 1983 (previously section 65 of the Mental Health Act 1959), and advises ministers accordingly. Because of its interest in patients under restriction orders, C3 was routinely informed of all findings of unfitness to plead in England and Wales prior to 1992,[1] and it had the task of finding an appropriate hospital for the unfit to plead defendant.

After being informed by a Crown Court of a finding of unfitness to plead, C3 would have approximately two months to find a hospital willing to admit the unfit to plead individual; if a bed could not be found within that time, under the terms of the CP(I)A 1964 the unfit to plead individual had to be released. Once the patient was admitted to hospital, C3 continued to monitor him or her as it would any patient under a restriction order, advising the minister in relation to requests for leave, transfer, discharge, or the lifting of restrictions. However, there was also the question of fitness to plead, and if fitness was recovered, a decision had to be made about whether or not the patient should be remitted to court for trial. A dossier, therefore, was gradually put together for each unfit to plead patient containing the information that was necessary to manage the case. This usually included a description of the alleged crime supplied by the police, the patient's antecedents and criminal record, contemporary psychiatric and social reports, regular progress reports by the responsible medical officer, notes on Home Office attitude to the case, and relevant correspondence. These records were the data source for the present study.

C3 made available to the author its files on all individuals found unfit to plead in England and Wales between 1976 and 1988. Access to the files was not restricted in any way, and documents outlining Home Office policies in relation to unfitness to plead were also seen. In cases where files were incomplete, an attempt was made to obtain further information from the hospital where the patient was sent, or from the relevant court.

Each file was evaluated by the author using a prepared checklist (see Appendix). The checklist was modified after a pilot phase in which the case notes relating to one year were examined; these 18 files were later re-examined using the final version of the checklist, and a comparison of similar items served as a partial check on test–retest reliability. In addition, two items—those relating to the severity of the offence and to the quality of evidence against the accused—were subjected to a test of inter-rater reliability. A colleague who had no connection with the project was asked to rate offence severity for 30 cases, and quality of evidence for 18 cases, using the scales devised for the study. Inter-rater reliability was found to be good: for severity $r = 0.85$, and for quality of evidence $r = 0.88$.

Information was collected about personal background, criminal and psychiatric histories, the alleged offence, mental state at both the time of the offence and the time of the trial, reasons for the finding of unfitness, disposal, treatment, progress, and outcome. Detailed notes were taken on each case in addition to the items coded, relating for instance to criminal record and psychiatric history, and these were coded at a later stage for computer analysis.

September 1989 was the last month for which follow-up information was obtained. The length of follow-up ranged, therefore, from 9 months to 13 years 9 months; where a file was reviewed early in 1989 and a change in the patient's status was possible, an update was obtained in September 1989 from the caseworker involved.

Data were coded and analysed by the author. Most of the initial analyses were carried out using SPSS-X (SPSS Inc., 1983), but subsidiary analyses were carried out with SPSS-PC+ (SPSS Inc., 1988).

Though each case reviewed for this study was in the public domain in the sense that the findings of unfitness to plead had all occurred in open court, many personal details about the defendants and information relating to their subsequent progress were not. Anonymity was therefore preserved in publications that resulted from the research, and it will continue to be preserved here.

NOTE

1. Since the Criminal Procedure (Insanity and Unfitness to Plead) Act came into force in January 1992, restriction orders have no longer been mandatory following an unfit to plead finding. From January 1992, therefore, C3 has only been advised of individuals found unfit to plead if they have also received a section 41 restriction order.

CHAPTER FIVE

Results

INTRODUCTION

Numbers: From 1976 to 1988 there were 295 findings of unfitness to plead in England and Wales documented by the Home Office. This is a slight under-representation of the actual number of findings over these years because records could not be found for a small number of cases involving minor offences where catchment area hospitals would not agree to admit the unfit to plead defendant. Because of the trivial nature of the alleged offence in these cases, it was not thought necessary by the Home Office to use its powers to direct admission to a reluctant hospital; instead, the individual was released directly from prison, and Home Office interest in the case ended after only a brief involvement. It is impossible to know precisely how many cases like this were missed, but from references to them in the files it is unlikely that there were more than three or four between 1976 and 1979; for reasons which will be discussed later this type of situation did not arise after 1980 (see p.67).

The number of findings of unfitness to plead declined significantly over the years of the study (Fig. 5.1). The mean number of findings per year for the entire 13-year period was 22.7, but the mean for the first 7 years was 28.7 (SD 9.6) compared with a mean of 15.7 (SD 2.6) for the next 6 years, a significant decrease ($t = 3.41$, $df = 11$, $P < 0.01$). The reason for this drop in the number of findings is unclear, but it can be

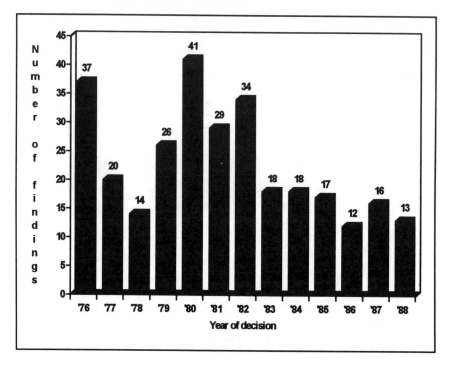

FIG. 5.1. Number of unfit to plead findings per year, 1976–1988 (*N* = 295).

seen in Fig. 5.2 that it was the continuation of a decline that had been
taking place for at least 40 years. During this period the number of
unfitness to plead findings, though fluctuating, fell by a factor of 4 to 5,
and the number of findings as a proportion of cases coming to trial in
the Crown Courts fell more smoothly and by a factor of 20 (*Criminal
Statistics* and Home Office documentation). Though he calculated the
number of cases in a different manner, it is clear from Walker (1968)
that the decline in unfitness findings in fact began in the years after the
First World War.

Over the years of the survey seven people were found unfit to plead
on two occasions, and one individual was found unfit to plead three times
(one man who appeared twice in this survey was also found unfit to plead
on two occasions in the early 1970s, giving him a possible record of four
unfit to plead findings). The 295 cases, therefore, involved 286
individuals.

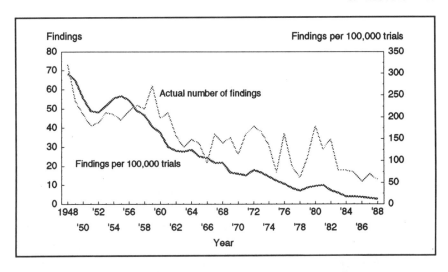

FIG. 5.2. The decline in findings of unfitness to plead since 1948, expressed in terms of the actual number of findings per year and as a proportion of Crown Court cases.

CHARACTERISTICS OF THE POPULATION

Sex, age, and ethnic origin: Individuals found unfit to plead in the years of the survey were predominantly male and in their 20s or 30s. Of the 286 individuals, 253 (88%) were male and 33 (12%) female; all those with multiple findings were male. The sex distribution was similar to that of the population as a whole that appeared before the Crown Courts over these years, where approximately 86% of defendants were male (*Criminal Statistics*). The mean age of defendants at the time of the 295 findings was 35.7 (SD 14.4, range 16–86), with a median age of 32; the age distribution is shown in Table 5.1. Though the mean age for females (40.0, SD 16.6) was higher than it was for males (35.1, SD 14.1), the difference was not statistically significant ($t = 1.62$, $df = 38$, $P = 0.11$).

Those found unfit to plead were thus from an older age group than other defendants appearing before the Crown Courts, at least if one compares them with those who were found guilty, where 40% of convicted defendants were under 20 years of age, and three-quarters were under 30 (Fig. 5.3).

The fact that the unfit to plead population is distributed over an older age range was not unexpected, as it is known that mentally ill offenders in general are older than other offender groups (Walker & McCabe, 1973). However, simple comparisons like this may be misleading

TABLE 5.1
Age distribution at time of finding (N = 295)

Age Range	Number	%
16–19	20	7
20–29	103	35
30–39	77	26
40–49	42	14
50–59	33	11
60+	20	7

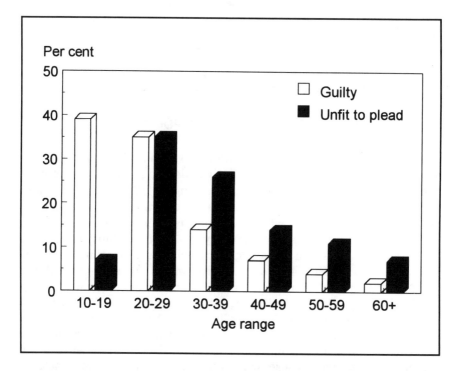

FIG. 5.3. Age distribution of those found guilty of indictable offences in 1982 (the mid-year of the survey) and those found unfit to plead (1976–1988). *Criminal Statistics for England and Wales* (1982).

because, although the majority of offenders do not reoffend, two-thirds of the unfit to plead population had previous convictions (see p.55); if one considered only individuals with previous convictions, therefore, the ages of the two groups might have been more similar.

Ethnic origin and place of birth were known for 283 of the 286 individuals (Table 5.2). Three-quarters of the population were Caucasian, of whom most (88%) were born in the United Kingdom (six others were born in Ireland). Most of the remainder were of Caribbean descent, the majority of whom (75%) were born outside the United Kingdom. None of those of Indian or Pakistani background, and only one individual of African origin, were born in the United Kingdom; overall, nearly 30% of those found unfit to plead were born outside the United Kingdom.

Criminal, psychiatric, and social factors: Two-thirds of the population already had a criminal record when they were found unfit to plead, and nearly a third had served at least one previous prison sentence; more than half had two or more previous convictions, one-fifth had been sentenced to prison at least twice, and nearly a quarter had received a hospital order from the courts in the past (Table 5.3). The median number of convictions for those with a criminal record was four. The figures are even higher for the 189 individuals who were psychotic at the time of the finding: 144 (76%) had at least one previous conviction, 117 (62%) had two or more previous convictions, and 72 (38%) had served a prison sentence, with a median of five convictions for those with a criminal record. On the other hand, 33 of the 59 mentally handicapped patients (56%) had *no* previous criminal record (though 16 (27%) did have 2 or more convictions and 7 (12%) had served a prison sentence); similarly, 7 of the 9 (78%) demented patients for whom the information was known had no criminal record.

Looking more closely at the interaction between previous prison and hospital disposals, 31 individuals (11%) had never been sentenced to prison but had received at least one hospital order from the courts in the past, 60 (21%) had been sentenced to prison but had never received

TABLE 5.2
Ethnic origin (data missing for 3 individuals)

Ethnic origin	Number	%
Caucasian	214	76
Caribbean	44	15
African	8	3
Indian subcontinent	12	4
Other	5	2
TOTAL	283	100

TABLE 5.3
Criminal background
(for those with multiple findings, background at first finding only included)

Criminal history	Number	%
Previous convictions (n = 281)		
None	92	33
Nonviolent only	145	52
Violent	44	16
Number of convictions (n = 278)		
None	92	33
One	40	14
Two	21	8
Three or more	125	45
Times in prison (n = 279)		
None	191	69
One	30	11
Two or more	58	21
Previous hospital order (n = 281)		
None	222	79
One	36	13
Two or more	23	9

a hospital order, and 28 (10%) had received at some time both a prison sentence and a hospital order, of whom a small number (9, 3%) had received two or more of each. The more previous convictions an individual had, the more likely it was that he or she had received at least one previous hospital order, with 7 (18%) of the 40 defendants with one conviction, 4 (19%) of the 21 with two convictions, 8 (42%) of the 19 with three convictions and 45 (40%) of the 114 with four or more convictions having been committed to hospital by the courts at some time in the past ($\chi^2 = 9.07$, $df = 3$, P < 0.05).

Clearly most of the population was no stranger to the criminal justice system. The vast majority of the population also had some previous contact with psychiatric services or, in the case of mental handicap, social services (Table 5.4). Over three-quarters of the sample had been in-patients on a psychiatric ward at some time in their lives, over a third had been committed to hospital at least once under a *civil* section of the Mental Health Act, and nearly 10% had been detained in hospital at different times under *both* civil and criminal sections of the Act; nearly half of those who had been in hospital had been there at least once nonvoluntarily. Less than a third of the population was actually receiving psychiatric care or supervision at the time of their alleged offences (a further 12% had defaulted from care in the previous six months), and more than one in ten were actually in-patients at the time

TABLE 5.4
Psychiatric background
(*n* = 286, except for "in-patient at offence", where *n* = 295 findings)

Psychiatric history	Number	%
Any previous contact	250	87
Previous admission ever	221	77
Civil section	101	35
Any section	140	49
Both criminal and civil sections	25	9
Unfit to plead (pre-1976)	9	3
In-patient at offence	42	14

(one of whom was already being detained because of a previous finding of unfitness to plead); 18 of these in-patients were mentally handicapped. For the 179 individuals who had a history of hospital admission but were not currently in-patients, the median number of months since their most recent discharge was 13.

Most of the population, therefore, had a degree of previous interaction with both mental health and criminal justice systems, some to quite an extent. Of the 277 individuals for whom the information was available, only 26 (9%) had neither a criminal record nor a history of hospital admission, whereas 156 (56%) had a history of both; 83 (30%) had two or more hospital admissions *and* two or more criminal convictions, 73 (26%) had been in hospital *and* had served a prison sentence, and 38 (14%) had been in both hospital *and* prison at least twice. Fifty-one (31%) of those with a diagnosis of schizophrenia had both three convictions and three hospital admissions. Most but not all of those in the sample who had previous convictions for violent offences (34 of 42; 81%) had been in hospital at least once.

A criminal record was less common in the females than it was in the males, with 16 (48%) of the 33 females having no previous convictions compared with 76 (30%) of the 253 males (χ^2 = 4.55, df = 1, P < 0.05). Furthermore, whereas 14 (42%) of the females had a history of hospital admissions but no previous convictions, this was true in just 51 (20%) of the males (χ^2= 8.24, df = 1, P < 0.01); on the other hand, whereas 30 of the males (12%) had a criminal record with no history of hospital admissions, this was not the case in any of the females.

Twenty three percent of cases (67) involved individuals who had no fixed abode (NFA) at the time of their alleged offences: 24% of the males in the population (N = 61) and 18% of the females (N = 6). A criminal record was more common in this group than it was in the rest of the sample, but this was due to a greater incidence of nonviolent offences; a history of violent offences was no more frequent in these individuals (Table 5.5). Though more of those of NFA had received hospital orders in the past than the nonNFA population, they were no more likely to have been detained under a civil section of the Mental Health Act or to have been detained in general in hospital against their will.

Employment was also not common among the population. Data were available for 272 individuals, of whom 220 (81%) were unemployed the year of their arrests, and a further 22 (8%) were either under 18 or retired. Thus, just 15 individuals (6%) were known to have been in regular work at the time of their alleged offences.

Diagnosis: A diagnosis was reached in each case based on the medical reports found in the files. In cases where a patient had more than one diagnosis, the one that appeared to be most responsible for the unfitness finding was counted as primary. In a case of schizophrenia and mental handicap, for instance, a diagnosis of schizophrenia was given if the patient was psychotic at the time of the trial and it was the psychosis that was responsible for the mental state that rendered the patient unfit to plead.

More than half the population had a primary diagnosis of schizophrenia, and about two-thirds had a primary diagnosis of some form of psychotic illness (Table 5.6). A quarter of the sample had a primary diagnosis of mental handicap or brain damage, but a further 14 individuals (5%) who also suffered from mental handicap or brain damage had been found unfit to plead for other reasons, including 4 of the 5 patients with a primary diagnosis of "deafness". Thus, about 30% of the population had some form of mental handicap or brain damage,

TABLE 5.5
Criminal and psychiatric characteristics broken down by NFA status

	NFA (n = 67)	nonNFA (n = 218)	χ^2	P
One conviction	59 (88%)	134 (61%)	16.58	0.001
3+ convictions	51 (76%)	71 (37%)	31.29	0.001
Previous prison	33 (49%)	31 (14%)	31.54	0.001
Violent conviction	13 (19%)	31 (14%)	1.05	0.300
Hospital order	26 (39%)	37 (17%)	14.19	0.001
Civil sect. of MHA	32 (48%)	83 (38%)	2.00	0.160
Any section	38 (57%)	102 (47%)	2.02	0.160
Any hospital admissions	53 (79%)	168 (77%)	0.12	0.730

TABLE 5.6
Primary diagnoses (N = 286)

Diagnosis	Number	%
Schizophrenia	164	57
Other psychosis	25	9
Dementia	10	3
Personal or neurotic disorder	11	4
Mental handicap	59	21
Brain damage	9	3
"Deaf"	5	2
None	3	1

but the degree of handicap was often not severe, at least if IQ is used as an indicator. The IQ was known for 48 of those with a primary diagnosis of mental handicap: In 14 (29%) the IQ was under 50, in 18 (38%) it was in the range of 50–59, in 15 (31%) it was in the range of 60–69, and in 1 case (2%) the IQ was above 70; the mean IQ in this group was 54.4 (SD 10.0).

The classic 19th-century cause of an unfit to plead finding, profound deafness combined with an inability to communicate, was present in only seven (2%) of the unfit to plead individuals in this survey: It was the primary cause of the unfitness finding in just five cases, while in two deaf patients the primary diagnosis was mental handicap. For the purposes of the Mental Health Act, these patients were classified as mentally impaired.

CHARACTERISTICS OF THE OFFENCE

Type of offence: Many individuals were charged with more than one offence. For analysis, only the most serious charge was considered (Table 5.7). The most common offences involved violence of some sort, accounting for two-thirds of the total. Fifty (17%) of all the alleged offences, 24 (26%) of the assaults, and 11 (39%) of the homicides involved family members of the accused.

Severity of offence: Offence type alone, however, means relatively little. Violent crimes, for instance, range from minor assault to homicide. Offences were therefore rated according to their severity using the following definitions.

TABLE 5.7
The alleged offences (N = 295)

Offence	Number	%
Assault	92	31
Theft	79	27
Arson	33	11
Sex offence	31	11
Homicide	28	9
Assault on police	11	4
Property damage	7	2
Possession of weapon	7	2
Other	7	2

Nuisance: Involved no physical risk to others and any property involved was of negligible worth (under £10 in value); for instance, stealing milk bottles from a doorstep, or breaking into a conservatory to sleep.

Mild: Any violence was of a minor nature, and property was valued at under £50; for instance, refusing to pay a taxi fare, or hitting out at a family member.

Moderate: Some injury could have or did occur but was not serious, or any property involved was valued up to a few thousand pounds; for instance, stealing a car, or threatening a police officer with a knife.

Severe: Substantial risk of physical injury or severe injury occurred, or property value was substantial; all homicides of course fell into this category.

It can be seen from Fig. 5.4 that severe offences accounted for about a quarter of all alleged offences, and nuisance and mild offences together made up about a third. Excluding homicide, the majority of assault offences were not of a severe nature, with 22% rated as nuisance or mild and 30% severe; of the thefts, 32% were rated as nuisance offences and a further 42% as mild, but none as severe.

Over the years of the survey there was an increase in the severity of offences allegedly committed by those found unfit to plead. From 1976 to 1982, 82 of the 201 offences (41%) were rated as nuisance or mild, and 39 (19%) were rated as severe; from 1983 to 1988, however, the proportion of nuisance or mild offences fell to 18 of 93 rateable offences

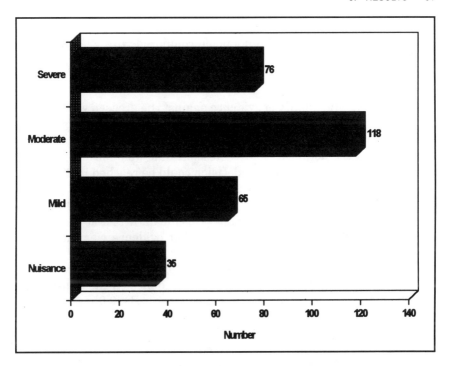

FIG. 5.4. Offence severity (one offence could not be rated).

(20%), and 37 offences (40%) were rated severe ($\chi^2 = 19.17$, $df = 2$, $P < 0.001$).

Offence severity was not associated with the sex or race of the offender: "Severe" offences were alleged to have been committed by 63 (25%) of the males compared with 12 (37%) of the females, and 59 (28%) of the white offenders compared with 16 (22%) of the non-Caucasians, differences which were not statistically significant. There were also no significant differences in relation to age, with the mean age of those accused of nuisance or mild offences being 36.0, compared with 34.0 for moderate, and 37.7 for severe offences.

It was of interest that though individuals of no fixed abode (NFA) formed about a quarter of the sample, they were responsible for 19 (54%) of the 35 nuisance offences, significantly more than would be expected by chance ($\chi^2 = 21.54$, $df = 1$, $P < 0.001$); indeed, 19 (28%) of the NFAs were accused of nuisance offences, compared with just 16 (7%) of the rest of the population. It was also of interest that the 27 individuals who had no criminal or psychiatric history were alleged to have committed a disproportionate number of severe offences, in particular homicide: Twelve (44%) were charged with offences rated as severe compared with

63 (24%) of the rest of the population ($\chi^2 = 5.06$, $df = 1$, $P < 0.05$), and 7 (25%) had been charged with homicide compared with 21 (8%) in the rest of the population ($\chi^2 = 8.79$, $df = 1$, $P < 0.01$).

Evidence: The quality of evidence against the accused was rated as clear or unclear based on the following criteria: presence of an eye witness; evidence found on the accused; forensic evidence linking the accused with the act; or a clear confession that was neither retracted nor challenged by the defence. A decision could be reached in 290 cases. Despite the relatively limited amount of information about offences contained in the files, the accused seemed to be clearly implicated in 83% of the alleged offences; frequently this meant arrest at the scene of the crime. It was of interest, however, that evidence was most often clear-cut for nuisance offences, where it was good in 33 of the 34 cases (97%), whereas it tended to be less clear in offences that were rated as severe, where in 58 (76%) of 76 cases the evidence on file appeared to clearly implicate the defendant ($\chi^2 = 8.96$, $df = 1$, $P < 0.05$).

INTERACTION OF THE DEFENDANT WITH THE JUDICIAL PROCESS

Admission of guilt: The file contained comment by the accused regarding his or her guilt or innocence in 206 cases (70%). In 17 (8%) of these cases the statements were contradictory or unclear, and in 49 (24%) the accused denied the charges, though often for psychotic reasons.[1] In 140 cases, however, (68% of those in which statements were found in the files, and 47% of all cases), the accused clearly admitted the charges. There was no association between admission of the act and the severity of the alleged offence ($\chi^2 = 3.73$, $df = 3$, $P = 0.79$), nor was there an association between admission and primary diagnosis ($\chi^2 = 9.97$, $df = 6$, $P = 0.13$).

There is special concern about confessions in relation to the mentally handicapped, but in this survey there were only seven cases in which mentally handicapped individuals found unfit to plead had confessed to offences where, given the available information, the evidence linking them to the offences was less than clear.

Mental state: Medical or psychiatric reports relating to the remand period were available in 290 cases. There was often more than one report for an individual, and in total 630 pre-trial reports produced by 182 prison medical officers, 446 psychiatrists, and 2 psychologists were seen (some of the doctors, of course, were involved in a number of different cases). In 400 (63%) of the reports it was clearly stated that the accused was unfit to plead, in 94 (15%) that the accused was fit to plead, and in 136 (22%) there was no comment in relation to fitness. Mental state can fluctuate, of course, but in 46 cases (16%) where an individual's mental state seemed to be similar when seen by different doctors, there was disagreement between them about that individual's fitness to plead; disagreement regarding fitness to plead was not associated with the diagnosis of the accused ($\chi^2 = 8.04$, $df = 6$, $P = 0.23$).

The various medical and psychiatric reports were used to gain an idea of the mental state of the population in the period leading up to the unfit to plead finding (Fig. 5.5). The most common findings in the mental state were thought disorder, delusions, paranoid ideas, and hallucinations.

In 86 cases (29%) there seemed to be a change in mental state between the alleged offence and the trial; in two cases defendants who would have been fit to plead made unsuccessful suicide attempts that left them brain damaged and unfit to plead. Fifteen of the 28 mute defendants (54%) had a primary diagnosis of psychosis, 4 (14%) had a primary diagnosis of mental handicap or brain damage, 1 had a primary

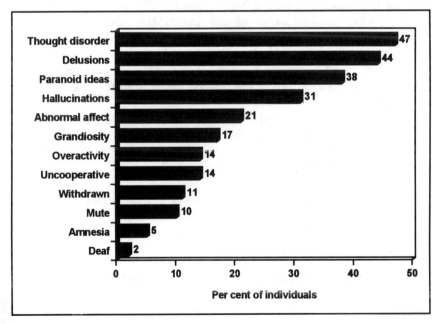

FIG. 5.5. Characteristics of the mental state while on remand (no data in 5 cases).

diagnosis of personality disorder and 1 was given no diagnosis; all 7 of the deaf defendants were mute and had only a limited ability to communicate. Though amnesia was mentioned in 14 cases (5%), it seemed to be the prime reason underlying the psychiatric recommendation for an unfit to plead finding in just 2 cases.

About a third of the population (102 individuals, 35%) had received at least some treatment pre-trial, usually consisting of medication in prison. Fifteen individuals (5%) were transferred to hospital for treatment on sections of the 1959 or 1983 Mental Health Acts during the remand period; in another 12 cases transfer to hospital under section had been attempted but could not be arranged, usually because of hospital resistance. It should be emphasised, however, that details about treatment pre-trial were extremely limited, and were not available at all in 30 cases.

Criteria for the recommendation: Reasons given by doctors in written reports for recommending that an individual be found unfit to plead are somewhat beside the point, as oral evidence led by a barrister is almost always given in court. In addition, the actual reason for the finding was rarely known as transcripts of court proceedings were not usually available; transcripts in any case would only have provided hints of the reasons behind a jury's decision. The medical reports do, however, give an indication of the psychiatric thinking behind a recommendation of unfitness to plead. The most common reasons given in reports were being unable to instruct legal advisers, being unable to comprehend court proceedings, and being unable to challenge a juror (Fig. 5.6). The distribution of the criteria listed in Fig. 5.6 was similar across diagnoses.

In addition to the standard criteria listed in Fig. 5.6, a variety of other reasons were suggested by doctors as to why an individual should be found unfit to plead. Some displayed an obvious confusion with the McNaughton criteria for insanity. For example:

"Although he admitted the incidents I was unable ... to determine whether he knew the offences were morally wrong. Moreover, it seems that he does not understand that assault is against the law";

"Although he is aware of the nature of his actions he is not able to view them in any sensible manner";

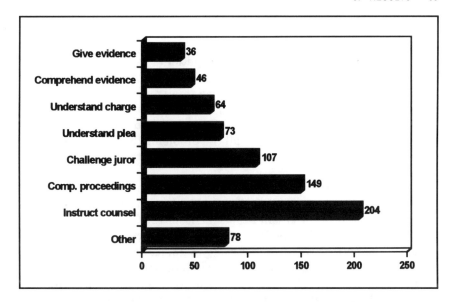

FIG. 5.6. Criteria given by reporting doctors to support a recommendation of unfitness to plead.

" . . . he is suffering from delusions which involve the police and therefore fundamentally affect his attitude to his alleged offence";

" . . . he cannot see any crime in what he has done".

Other criteria that were put forward included "a lack of insight into delusional thinking", "being unable to appreciate the imposition of a sentence", and "not being able to conform with court protocol". Other less orthodox reasons included:

"He is often not truthful . . . and his statements would be misleading";

"This man is not fit to plead, not because of subnormality *per se* but because he is functioning and living in a fantasy and cuckoo world";

"He cannot conduct a reasonable, sensible conversation";

"He won't accept the jurisdiction of the court".

OUTCOME

Hospital disposal: The majority of patients were admitted to local psychiatric hospitals, with under a third sent to one of the maximum security special hospitals (Table 5.8). In a small number of cases patients were sent to a special hospital not on grounds of security or clinical need, but because the catchment area hospital refused admission and, rather than direct admission there with all the problems that would be sure to follow, the Home Office arranged for admission to a special hospital through the DHSS.

All 10 of the individuals who were suffering from dementia were sent to local hospitals, as were 4 of the 5 individuals with a primary diagnosis of deafness (the other was sent to special hospital). Otherwise, diagnosis was not associated with the type of hospital (in terms of security level) to which the patient was transferred (χ^2 = 18.41, df = 12, P = 0.10): For instance, 61 (31%) of the 189 psychotic individuals were sent to special hospitals, as were 18 (31%) of the 59 mentally handicapped patients and 5 (46%) of the 11 personality disordered patients. The sex of the offender was also not associated with the type of hospital to which he or she was sent, with 9 (28%) of the females and 79 (31%) of the males admitted to special hospitals (χ^2 = 0.14, df = 2, P = 0.93).

It was not surprising that the severity of the alleged offence was associated with hospital disposal, with 50 (67%) of the 75 individuals involved in offences rated as severe being sent to special hospitals compared with 31 (28%) of the 112 accused of moderate offences and 7 (7%) of the 98 accused of nuisance or mild offences (χ^2 = 87.83, df = 4, P < 0.001); despite this, however, it can be seen in Fig. 5.7 that the different types of hospital all received patients who had been accused of all levels of offence severity.

Nine individuals were not admitted to hospital at all: Six were said to have regained fitness to plead while still in prison and were returned directly to court for trial, and three were simply discharged from prison

TABLE 5.8
Hospital disposal

Hospital	Number	%
Local	170	58
Medium security	30	10
Special hospital	88	30
None	9	3

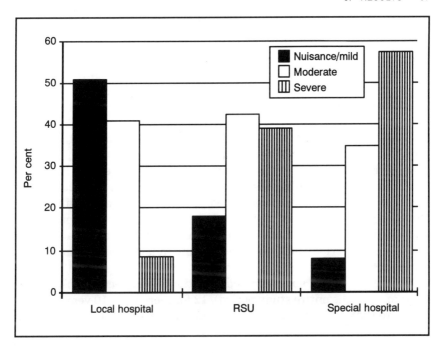

FIG. 5.7. Severity of alleged offence and hospital disposal; cases not sent to hospital excluded (*N* = 285).

once the two-month period during which hospital transfer must occur had lapsed. In a further 18 cases involving trivial offences where hospitals expressed reluctance to admit the unfit to plead individual because of the associated restriction order, a special warrant was created which in effect removed restrictions on discharge as soon as they were created. This evolved because legal advice to the Home Office suggested that restrictions on discharge could not be waived *prior* to admission as the patient would not yet be under the provisions of the Mental Health Act; transfer, therefore, had to take place with restrictions in place. The special warrant stated that though admission was under the provisions of the CP(I)A 1964, restrictions would be terminated as soon as the patient was admitted. Fifteen of the special warrant cases involved psychotic individuals, two were mentally handicapped, and one was a patient with senile dementia.

In 1980, policy was reviewed in relation to unfit to plead individuals charged with petty offences. It was decided that discharge from prison without transfer to hospital should no longer take place, and that the use of the special warrant should cease. The Home Office took the view that the CP(I)A 1964 required the Home Secretary to direct admission to hospital, and that to do otherwise would negate the provisions of the Act. Thus, from 1980 all unfit to plead individuals were admitted to hospital with restrictions in place regardless of offence severity, though in trivial cases where public safety was not an issue the Home Office often let it be known that the early removal of restrictions would be considered favourably.

Long-term outcome: As of the end of September 1989, the population could be split into four main, more or less equal, outcome groups (Fig. 5.8): Those who returned for trial, those who had been conditionally or absolutely discharged, those for whom restrictions had been lifted, and those who continued to be detained in hospital under the CP(I)A 1964. A small number of cases resulted in other outcomes, such as death or deportation. Two individuals still detained at the end of the survey period had trials pending, and in fact appeared in court in early 1990.

By the end of the survey period, 5 patients had been in hospital for 12 years (i.e. the entire study period), 12 for more than 10 years, and 47 for more than 5 years. Of the 212 patients who were no longer detained

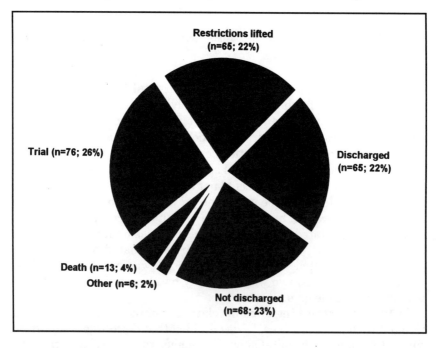

FIG. 5.8. Outcome (one patient found unfit to plead three times without ever being discharged is counted only once; *N* = 293).

in hospital under the Act (excluding the 13 who died and the 6 with "other" outcomes), 118 (56%) had been discharged from the provisions of the Act within one year, and 150 (71%) within two years.

For those who did not return to court, the time between the initial finding and eventual discharge from the provisions of the Act reflected the severity of the alleged offence. The mean time until discharge from the CP(I)A in this group (excluding the 18 patients admitted under special warrants and the 6 with "other" outcomes) was 34.1 months (SD 36.0), but those accused of nuisance or mild offences were detained for an average of 17.5 months (SD 19.2), those accused of moderate offences for 43.2 months (SD 35.5) and those accused of severe offences for 69.8 months (SD 52.5) (F = 17.5, df = 2, P < 0.001). Thus, those accused of the most serious offences who were eventually discharged without trial were detained under the Act for about four times as long as those who were alleged to have committed the least serious offences.

As described earlier (p.52), seven individuals were found unfit to plead on two occasions over the years of the survey, and one was found unfit three times. The man with three findings had been charged with two further offences without ever having been discharged from the provisions of the Act or from hospital after his first finding; in the other seven cases, three had been tried following their first unfitness findings, two had had their restrictions lifted, and two had been given conditional or absolute discharges.

Recovery of fitness: Once the unfit to plead defendant became a patient, it was up to the responsible medical officer (RMO) to decide whether or not fitness was recovered. In total, 135 patients (46%) were declared fit to plead by their RMOs, and 160 (54%) remained unfit. However, recovery of fitness was not an issue in the 18 individuals who were admitted to hospital on special warrants allowing for their immediate discharge from the conditions of the Act (see p.66), and if they are excluded the percentage who regained their fitness increases to 49%. In a further 56 patients who had not formally been declared fit to plead (19% of the total but 35% of the unrecovered group), it seemed likely from medical or tribunal reports that fitness had in fact been regained, but the RMO had not been asked to comment specifically about this and the doctor did not raise the issue spontaneously.[2] Altogether, therefore, it seemed that just 84 patients (28%) had not regained their fitness to plead.

Though recovery of fitness was associated with diagnosis (107 (59%) of the 181 patients with a primary diagnosis of psychosis recovered their fitness compared with 12 (21%) of the 57 with a diagnosis of mental handicap;[3] (x^2 = 25.12, df = 1, P < 0.001), it is notable that a fifth of the mentally handicapped had recovered their capacity to plead, and in a further 7 cases (12%) this seemed probable. Recovery in those with mental handicap was not simply due to improvement in a concomitant psychosis, as only 1 of the 12 mentally handicapped patients who had recovered their fitness to plead had a secondary diagnosis of psychosis, as did only 1 of the 7 cases where recovery was considered probable. Thus, in about a third of the mentally handicapped patients, where a change in fitness status might be thought unlikely, fitness appeared to have been regained.

In the 135 cases where fitness was recovered, the average time between the initial finding and the RMO advising the Home Office that the patient had become fit to plead was 10.5 months. The range in time was wide, from almost nil in cases where the RMO disagreed with the finding, to nearly 12 years, but in total, 82% of those who became fit did so within a year. In view of this skewed distribution, the median time to recovery of fitness, which was 4 months, is probably a more meaningful figure. It should be emphasised that these figures are an overestimate of the time taken to regain fitness as there was inevitably a delay between the RMO deciding that the patient had regained his or her fitness to plead and the Home Office being informed of this opinion. It should also be noted that the figures given here are calculated from when the decision was reached in court, and take no account of the delay before admission to hospital could take place.

Not surprisingly, outcome differed depending on whether or not a patient was said to have recovered fitness capacity (Table 5.9). Of those who regained their fitness, the majority returned to court, and most of the rest were no longer detained under the CP(I)A, with only about 10% still in hospital under the conditions of the Act by the end of the survey. The 41 patients (excluding those with "other" outcomes) who had

TABLE 5.9
Outcome by fitness status

Status	Recovers fitness (n = 135)	Remains unfit (n = 158)
Remains in hospital	15 (11%)	53 (34%)
Conditional/Absolute discharge	27 (20%)	38 (24%)
Restrictions lifted	14 (10%)	51 (32%)
Trial	76 (56%)	0
Death	1 (1%)	12 (8%)
Other	2 (2%)	4 (3%)

recovered their fitness and who were discharged from the provisions of the Act *without* returning to court were detained for a mean of 30.9 months (SD 36.8), and a median of 16 months; those still detained despite recovering their fitness had been in hospital for an average of 5.4 years.

In comparison, though many of those who *had not recovered their fitness* had also been discharged from hospital or had their restrictions lifted, a third were still detained in hospital under the Act. The 88 who were no longer detained (excluding those with "other" outcomes) had been held under the provisions of the Act for a mean of 36.0 months (SD 35.7), and a median of 25 months. The mean length of detention for those who were discharged from the Act without regaining their fitness did not differ significantly from that for individuals who had regained their fitness but who were discharged without returning to court ($t = 0.71$, $df = 109$, $P = 0.48$).

In the subgroup of 56 patients who were not formally declared fit to plead but who had probably become so, 12 (21%) were still detained in hospital under the provisions of the Act at the end of the survey period, the average length of detention being 7.2 years. The mean time taken to recover fitness in this group was 26.0 months, with a median of 12.5 months.

Thirteen patients died in hospital while still detained as unfit to plead. Six were patients with senile dementia, two were patients with probable alcoholic brain damage, and two were elderly schizophrenic patients. The remaining three deaths were in younger schizophrenic patients and occurred within one year of the unfit to plead finding: Two were by suicide and one was from an unknown cause.

Under the Mental Health Act 1959, tribunals could make recommendations about the discharge of restriction order patients, but they could not actually order their discharge. Only two of the 39 patients who had been seen by tribunals under the 1959 Act and who were still detained under the CP(I)A at the end of the survey period had been unsuccessfully recommended for discharge by a tribunal. Since the Mental Health Act 1983, tribunals have had the power to discharge patients held under restriction orders, including those detained under the CP(I)A (though they are not empowered to rule on whether or not a patient has become fit to plead). Between January 1984 and September 1989, tribunals discharged 25 unfit to plead patients, 22 conditionally and 3 absolutely; 7 (28%) of these patients had been accused of offences rated as severe. Less than half the discharged patients (11, 44%) had been declared fit to plead by their RMOs, though another 7 had probably become fit to plead by the time of their tribunal hearings.

PATIENTS STILL DETAINED

The sample was divided into two groups depending on whether or not they were still detained in hospital under the provisions of the CP(I)A. Those found unfit to plead in 1988, the last year of the survey, were excluded in order to ensure that the follow-up period was of a reasonable length, i.e. at least 21 months. Thus, only those found unfit to plead between 1976 and 1987 were included in this part of the analysis. In the seven individuals with multiple findings, the outcome in relation to the final finding only was used; those who had died or who had received an outcome of "other" were also excluded. This left 254 individuals, of whom 63 were still detained in hospital under the provisions of the Act, and 191 who were not (though they may of course have remained in hospital under other provisions of the Mental Health Act).

Diagnosis: Mental handicap as a primary diagnosis was much more common in those who were still detained in hospital under the Act, occurring in 25 patients (40%) in this group compared with 31 (16%) of the patients who were no longer detained (χ^2 = 15.16, df = 1, P < 0.001). Looked at in another way, 45% of patients whose primary diagnosis was mental handicap continued to be detained in hospital under the Act, compared with 23% of schizophrenics (34 of 147), none of the 11 patients with psychoses other than schizophrenia, just 1 of the 7 patients with brain damage, 1 of the 11 with personality disorders, and 1 of the 5 patients who were deaf.

Sex, ethnic origin, and age: Patients who were still detained in hospital under the CP(I)A did not differ significantly in terms of their sex or ethnic origins from those who were no longer detained: 57 (91%) of those still detained were male compared with 166 (87%) of those no longer detained (χ^2 = 0.56, df = 1, P = 0.45), and 17 (27%) of those still detained were of non-Caucasian backgrounds compared with 50 (26%) of the nondetained group (χ^2 = 0.02, df = 1, P = 0.90). Though those still detained were a younger group, having a mean age of 31.5 (SD 12.1) at the time of the finding compared with a mean age of 35.7 (SD 13.6) in the nondetained group (t = 2.36, df = 252, P < 0.05), if the greater number of mentally handicapped patients (who are a younger group, see p.81) in the still detained group is controlled for, the age difference between detained and no longer detained patients disappears.

Psychiatric and criminal histories: Psychiatric histories among those in each group were similar in respect of the frequency of hospital admissions, both of a voluntary and a compulsory nature (Table 5.10).

TABLE 5.10
Criminal, psychiatric background by detention status

	Detained (n = 63)	No longer detained (n = 191)	χ^2	P
Criminal record (not known = 4)			6.57	0.040
None	26 (42%)	55 (29%)		
Nonviolent only	24 (39%)	108 (57%)		
Violent	12 (19%)	25 (13%)		
Psychiatric admissions (not known = 6)			4.02	0.260
None	8 (13%)	40 (22%)		
1–2	23 (37%)	56 (30%)		
3 or more	31 (50%)	90 (48%)		
Any MHA admission	49 (52%)	92 (48%)	1.03	0.310
Long-term patient	16 (26%)	4 (2%)	32.32	0.001
In-patient at offence	23 (37%)	13 (7%)	33.90	0.001

However, significantly more of the detained group were in-patients at the time of their alleged offences, and more were already long-term hospital patients, the majority because of mental handicap: Just 14% of the population (42 individuals) were in-patients at the time of their alleged offences, but in-patients accounted for 37% of all those still detained under the Act, and 23 (55%) of the 42 in-patients were still detained. The groups also differed in terms of their criminal backgrounds, with those still detained less likely to have had a criminal record, but the difference disappears if the greater number of mentally handicapped patients in the still detained group is controlled.

Offence: Patients still detained were more likely to have been accused of a violent offence, and an offence that was rated as severe (Table 5.11), with nearly half of those patients still detained charged with a severe offence compared with under a fifth of those who had been discharged from the provisions of the Act; nearly a fifth had been charged with homicide compared with just over 5% of those who were no longer detained.

Looking at Table 5.11 in a slightly different way, just 8% of those accused of theft or property damage remained detained under the Act, compared with 29% of the allegedly violent offenders, 48% of the sex offenders and 52% of the patients charged with homicide; 48% of those charged with severe offences remained detained compared with 13% of those accused of nuisance or mild offences and 21% of those accused of offences rated of moderate severity. Almost half of those still detained

TABLE 5.11
Detention status by offence type and severity

Offence	Detained (n = 63)	No longer detained (n = 191)
Type[1]		
Theft or property damage	6 (10%)	71 (37%)
Weapon or violence		
(excluding homicide)	27 (43%)	66 (35%)
Homicide	12 (19%)	11 (6%)
Sex offence	13 (21%)	14 (7%)
Arson	5 (8%)	24 (13%)
Other	0	5 (3%)
Severity[2]		
Nuisance/mild	11 (17%)	80 (42%)
Moderate	22 (35%)	81 (42%)
Severe	30 (48%)	33 (17%)

[1] $\chi^2 = 32.50$, $df = 5$, $P < 0.001$.
[2] $\chi^2 = 25.38$, $df = 2$, $P < 0.001$.

under the Act (30, 48%) had initially been sent to a special hospital compared with about a quarter (49, 27%) of the group that was no longer detained ($\chi^2 = 10.67$, $df = 1$, $P < 0.01$); this was probably a reflection of the more serious nature of their offences.

It has already been mentioned that evidence linking the accused with the crime was good in the majority of cases (p.62). In the group still detained, however, evidence tended to be clear less often, being clear-cut in 47 (75%) of cases compared with 165 (87%) in the group that was no longer detained under the Act ($\chi^2 = 5.05$, $df = 1$, $P < 0.05$); again, however, the difference disappears when the greater number of mentally handicapped patients among the detained group is controlled (see p.81).

Progress: Forty-six (73%) of the patients still detained under the Act remained in the same hospital to which they had initially been sent. Thirteen (21%) of this group had been declared fit to plead by their RMOs, and a further 11 (18%) had probably become so. Of the 34 still detained patients with a primary diagnosis of mental illness, 22 (65%) remained acutely psychotic, and of the 25 still detained mentally impaired patients, 19 (76%) continued to display serious behavioural problems at least occasionally. In only five cases where the RMO had requested that restrictions should be lifted had this not occurred by the end of the survey period, though often this took much longer than the RMO would have liked.

TRIAL

Policy: If a patient recovers fitness to plead, the Home Secretary can remit the individual back to prison to await trial. Before 1982, however, Home Office policy in relation to remission for trial meant that such remissions were far from routine.[5] The general principle was that an accused person ought to have an opportunity to demonstrate his or her innocence in court, but this was balanced against the question of whether any useful purpose would in fact be served by having a trial.

In general, four factors were said to favour remission: If there was real doubt about the patient's guilt, if the patient was thought to have feigned mental disorder, if the court or prosecuting authority had expressed a view that the patient should be tried if fitness was recovered, or if the patient expressed a clear desire for a trial. In most cases, however, these factors were outweighed by other considerations: If mounting a trial would be difficult given the time elapsed since the alleged offence (one year tended to be the upper limit), if the likely outcome of a trial would be a hospital order with restrictions (meaning that the patient's status in hospital would in effect remain unchanged), if the patient had already been in hospital for as long as the relevant sentence, if the alleged offence was trivial, or if a resumption of proceedings carried a high risk of causing the patient's relapse. In practice, the first two considerations were usually most relevant.

In 1982 this policy was changed so that in cases where fitness to plead was recovered, remission for trial was to be the rule rather than the exception; a finding of unfitness to plead was to be considered a postponement of trial, not a cancellation. From 1982 it was assumed that a trial would take place unless their were good reasons for it not to go ahead.

Numbers: Not surprisingly, the result of the change in policy described was a marked increase in the proportion of unfit to plead patients who were remitted for trial (Fig. 5.9). By the end of the survey period in September 1989, 76 individuals had returned to court, of whom only 14 (18%) were tried before 1982; of those found unfit to plead prior to 1982, 20 (12%) of 167 were eventually tried, compared with 56 (44%) of the 128 found unfit to plead from that year ($\chi^2 = 38.25$, $df = 1$, $P < 0.001$).

Time variables: On average, in those who returned for trial the Home Office was notified that fitness to plead had been recovered 7.1

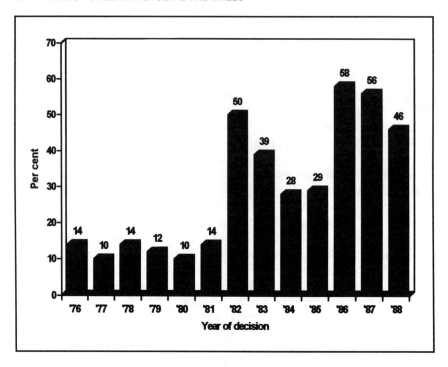

FIG. 5.9. Percentage of cases coming to trial.

months (SD 12.4) after the initial unfit to plead finding, and a median of 4 months after the finding; by 6 months 54 (74%) of the patients had recovered their fitness to plead and by a year 67 (88%) had. The mean length of time between the original finding and eventual trial was 14.2 months (SD 16.5), with a range of 3 months to 8.5 years (two trials took place more than 8 years after the initial finding); the median time between finding and trial was 10 months. The average time between arrest and eventual trial was 19.1 months (SD 17.1), with a median of 14 months; just 28% of those who were returned to court (21 patients) had their definitive trials within a year of their arrest.

Trial outcome: The verdict in the large majority of trials was one of guilt (Fig. 5.10). Though more than half of those who were found guilty were given hospital orders, over a quarter received a noncustodial sentence involving neither hospital nor prison detention, such as a suspended sentence or a probation order (Fig. 5.11). If those who were found not guilty or who were not proceeded against are included, then 37% emerged from trial free from either hospital or prison detention.

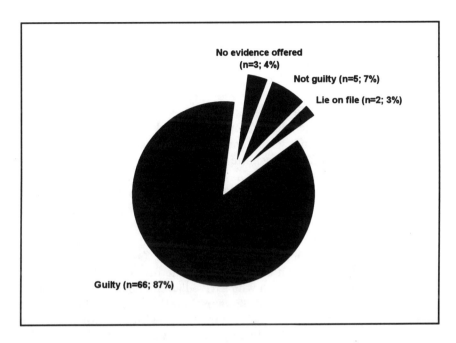

FIG. 5.10. Trial outcome (*N* = 76).

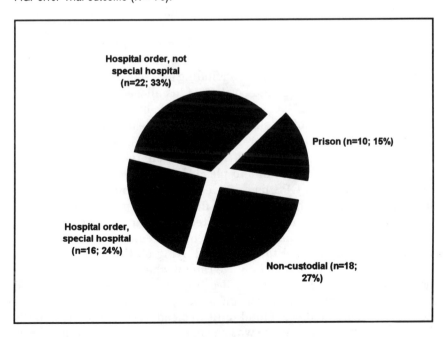

FIG. 5.11. Sentences for those found guilty (*N* = 66).

Ten (45%) of the 22 hospital orders that did not involve detention in a special hospital included a restriction order, whereas only 1 (6%) of the 16 hospital orders that were to a special hospital did not have a restriction order attached. Three of the prison sentences were for a year or less, five were from one to five years, one was between five and ten years, and one was a life sentence.

The five cases in which defendants were found not guilty involved two thefts, one assault, one sex offence and one case of arson. All five defendants suffered from psychotic illnesses at the time of the unfit to plead finding. Fitness to plead was recovered in an average of just 2.2 months in these five individuals, all had recovered their fitness to plead within four months, and four of the five patients were back in court within one year of the initial unfit to plead finding.

In only one of the not guilty cases, however, did the verdict seem to reflect clearly the innocence of the accused (see pp.95–96 for a description of this case). Of the other four, the first (case 174) involved a homeless schizophrenic man who arrived at the house of his parents, demanded food and then hit his 82-year-old father over the head with a candlestick. He admitted the act, saying that he hit his father because he was "avaricious"; found unfit to plead, he was acquitted 16 months later, possibly because of his father's reluctance to testify against his son. The second case (221) was of a schizophrenic man charged with stealing money from the client of a prostitute, the victim himself having been accused of stealing the money from the prostitute in the first place. Found unfit to plead against medical advice, he was returned to court eight months after the unfit to plead finding and was acquitted, possibly because of the less than sound position of his alleged victim. The third case (257) involved a 27-year-old schizophrenic man who was accused, along with six others, of breaking into a house. He admitted the offence at the time, but he failed to surrender to bail and disappeared to France. He was re-arrested three years later, but on remand was acutely psychotic and was found unfit to plead. He was brought to trial five months later, but the CPS had decided it was no longer in the public interest to proceed with the case and a finding of not guilty was returned without the facts ever having been tested. The fourth case (258) was of a 23-year-old mentally handicapped, schizophrenic man charged with pulling a 15-year-old girl to the ground, lying on top of her and then touching her breasts and vagina. He ran off when she hit him over the head with her shoe. He told the police at the time that he had intended to "take her money and have it off with her". On remand he became acutely psychotic and was found unfit to plead. At his trial six months later he insisted that the case was one of mistaken identity and he was acquitted because of doubt about the evidence.

Factors associated with trial: Patients who were remitted for trial tended to be younger than those who were not remitted, even when patients with a diagnosis of senile dementia are excluded: The mean age at the initial finding for those who were tried was 31.9 (SD 10.8) compared with a mean age of 35.4 (SD 13.3) in those who were not ($t = 2.27$, $df = 277$, $P < 0.05$). Overall, trial was more likely if the alleged offence was of a moderate or severe nature, if the patient had a criminal record, if the diagnosis was one of mental illness rather than mental handicap or brain damage, if the patient was from an ethnic minority, or if the patient was sent to a medium or maximum security hospital rather than to a local hospital (Table 5.12). It was of interest that the quality of evidence against the accused did not appear to influence whether or not remission for trial took place.

The 1982 policy modification that led to an increase in the number of remissions for trial was associated with a change in who was remitted

TABLE 5.12
Trial status by patient and offence characteristics (excluding 4 individuals with multiple findings who were not tried, and 2 cases with trials pending; N = 289)

	No trial (n = 213)	Trial (n = 76)	χ^2	P
Sex			0.08	0.78
Male	188 (73%)	68 (27%)		
Female	25 (76%)	8 (24%)		
Ethnic origin			7.48	0.01
Caucasian	166 (78%)	47 (22%)		
Non-Caucasian	47 (62%)	28 (38%)		
Criminal record			17.11	0.001
None	82 (88%)	11 (12%)		
Nonviolent only	100 (68%)	47 (32%)		
Violent	26 (59%)	18 (41%)		
In-patient at offence	34 (85%)	6 (15%)	3.19	0.07
Offence severity			5.87	0.05
Nuisance/mild	81 (82%)	17 (17%)		
Moderate	80 (69%)	36 (31%)		
Severe	52 (70%)	22 (30%)		
Unclear evidence	27 (64%)	15 (36%)	2.20	0.14
Hospital			20.42	0.001
Local	141 (84%)	26 (16%)		
Medium security	15 (54%)	13 (46%)		
Special hospital	55 (64%)	31 (36%)		
Diagnosis			17.76	0.001
Mental illness	128 (66%)	65 (34%)		
Mental handicap	63 (93%)	5 (7%)		

for trial, and an increase in the speed with which remission occurred. After 1982 the ethnic origin of the patient, the severity of the alleged offence, and the type of hospital to which the patient was sent were no longer associated with the likelihood of remission for trial (Table 5.13). And though the differences did not quite reach statistical significance, the time between the initial finding and eventual trial tended to be reduced for those who were found unfit to plead after 1982, as was the time between arrest and eventual trial (Table 5.14).

MENTAL ILLNESS VERSUS MENTAL HANDICAP

In 189 cases the finding of unfitness to plead was associated with a psychotic illness, whereas in 59 cases the finding related to a primary diagnosis of mental handicap. Ten of the mentally handicapped patients also had an associated psychotic illness.

TABLE 5.13
Trial status by ethnic origin, offence severity, and hospital, 1982–1988 (N = 55)

	No trial	Trial	χ^2	P
Ethnic origin			1.36	0.30
Caucasian	54 (59%)	38 (41%)		
Non-Caucasian	16 (47%)	18 (53%)		
Offence severity			2.39	0.30
Nuisance/mild	19 (59%)	13 (41%)		
Moderate	25 (48%)	27 (52%)		
Severe	26 (63%)	15 (37%)		
Hospital			4.29	0.12
Local	42 (67%)	21 (33%)		
Medium security	11 (46%)	13 (54%)		
Special hospital	17 (50%	17 (50%)		

TABLE 5.14
Time variables in those remitted for trial
(group 1: unfit to plead 1976–1981, n = 20;
group 2: unfit to plead 1982–1988, n = 56)

	Group 1 mean (months)	Group 2 mean (months)	t	P
Finding to recovery	13.4 (SD 22.3)	5.0 (SD 5.0)	1.63	0.12
Finding to trial	23.3 (SD 27.9)	10.9 (SD 6.7)	1.90	0.07
Arrest to trial	27.8 (SD 28.3)	15.8 (SD 8.0)	1.83	0.08

Patient characteristics:[6]   Compared with psychotic defendants, the mentally handicapped were younger at the time of the finding, with a mean age of 28.5 (SD 12.5) as opposed to a mean age of 36.1 (SD 12.4) in the psychotic patients (t = 4.08, df = 246, P < 0.001); 22 (37%) of the mentally handicapped patients were under 20 years of age compared with just 8 (4%) of those who were psychotic. The mentally handicapped were also more likely to be white: 90% of the mentally handicapped (53 individuals) were of Caucasian background compared with 70% (132 individuals) of the psychotic defendants (χ^2 = 9.48, df = 1, P < 0.01).

The mentally handicapped had less previous involvement with the criminal justice system than did the psychotic patients (see also p.55), but their overall younger age needs to be taken into account. Fifty-six percent of the mentally handicapped patients (33 individuals) had no criminal record compared with 24% of the psychotic defendants (45 individuals; χ^2 = 21.52, df = 1, P < 0.001). However, 51% of the mentally handicapped (30 individuals) were actively involved with either psychiatric or social services at the time of their alleged offences compared with 22% of the 184 psychotic defendants for whom this information was known (41 individuals; χ^2 = 17.63, df = 1, P < 0.001). Moreover, 31% of the mentally handicapped (18 individuals) were actually in-patients at the time of their alleged offences compared with 10% (18 individuals) of the psychotic patients (χ^2 = 14.03, df = 1, P < 0.001).

Among those who were psychotic, 151 (83%) of 182 for whom this information was known had at least one previous psychiatric admission, and 103 (56%) had three or more; among the mentally handicapped, 43 (73%) of 59 had at least one admission, but just 17 (29%) had three or more, though it must of course be remembered that they were a younger group.

Offence characteristics: Similar proportions of the two groups were charged with offences rated as mild, moderate or severe, but psychotic defendants were more often charged with offences rated of nuisance severity: 28 (15%) of the psychotic defendants compared with just 2 (3%) of the mentally handicapped were charged with nuisance offences (χ^2 = 4.50, df = 1, P < 0.05). However, this difference was largely accounted for by the excess of psychotic patients among those of NFA, in whom nuisance offences were over-represented (see pp.57–58 & 61): Only 1 of the 67 NFA individuals was mentally handicapped, compared with 59 psychotic individuals.

In cases involving the mentally handicapped, the evidence in the files linking them with the offence was less strong, rated clear-cut in 39 (67%) of 58 rateable offences compared with 168 (91%) of 185 rateable offences where the accused was psychotic (χ^2 = 19.44, df = 1, P < 0.001). The mentally handicapped were also more likely to have been accused of sexual offences, and less likely to have been accused of assaults short of homicide (Fig. 5.12).

It has already been mentioned that the recovery of fitness was associated with diagnosis (p.69), with 59% of those with some form of psychosis recovering their fitness to plead compared with 21% of the mentally handicapped. However, only 4 (7%) of the mentally handicapped were remitted for trial compared with 62 (33%) of the psychotic patients; all 4 of the mentally handicapped defendants who returned to court were found guilty.

Outcome: Similar proportions of each group were sent to each of the three types of hospital, with about 30% from both groups going to special hospitals. However, nearly a half of the mentally handicapped who were not remitted for trial were still detained in hospital under the conditions

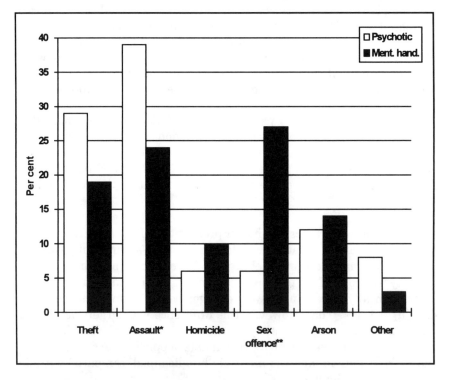

FIG. 5.12. Offence type by psychotic (N = 189) or mental handicap (N = 59).
* Assault: psychotic N = 73; mental handicap N = 14, χ^2 = 4.38, df = 1, P < 0.05
** Sex offence: psychotic N = 12, mental handicap N = 16; χ^2 = 19.37, df = 1, P < 0.001.

of the Act, compared with less than a third of those with some form of psychosis: 27 (49%) of 55 mentally handicapped individuals found unfit to plead before 1988 were still detained compared with 35 (21%) of 115 psychotic individuals ($\chi^2 = 5.38$, $df = 1$, $P < 0.05$). It should be noted, however, that 14 of the still detained mentally handicapped patients, that is, more than half, had been in-patients at the time of their alleged offences, and 10 of these 14 were already long-term hospital patients.

Discharge from the conditions of the Act for those who were not remitted for trial tended to be longer for patients with mental handicap, with a mean of 37.4 months (SD 37.3) in the 28 mentally handicapped patients compared with a mean of 24.7 months (SD 30.3) in the 89 discharged psychotic patients, but this difference did not reach statistical significance ($t = -1.83$, $df = 115$, $P = 0.07$).

NOTES

1. For instance, one man who was accused of seriously injuring his parents admitted the act but denied his guilt on the grounds that his acts were controlled by laser beams from outer space.
2. Only recently has the Home Office inquired into a patient's fitness status as a matter of routine. Previously the issue tended to be raised only if a trial was being considered, or if a relatively early discharge was requested.
3. These figures exclude the 18 patients admitted on special warrants.
4. If the 18 patients who were admitted on special warrants are included, then the mean period of detention falls to 29.3 months (SD 34.9) and a median of 12 months.
5. Policy in relation to remission for trial was referred to in a number of files; the clearest pre-1982 statement of policy can be found in file MNP 2/926/2.
6. The first finding only is considered in cases of multiple findings for patient descriptions, the final finding only where outcome is described.

CHAPTER SIX

Discussion

THE RATIONALE FOR THE FINDING

In contrast to the 20 or so unfit to plead findings that took place annually over the years of the survey, the annual number of hospital orders issued by the courts over the same years ranged from 700 to 800 (Dell, Grounds, James, & Robertson, 1991). Many more mentally disordered defendants would have been dealt with through conditional discharges, probation orders, prison sentences, and a variety of other disposals, and others would have been diverted from the criminal justice system well before the question of sentencing even arose. Do, therefore, those individuals who travel the unfit to plead route differ in any important respects from the majority of mentally disordered defendants who negotiate the criminal justice system each year?

Certainly the unfit to plead population itself was no stranger to the courts or court processes. About two-thirds of those found unfit to plead in this survey had been before the courts previously, been considered fit to plead, and had been convicted and sentenced, with more than half the sample having been dealt with by the courts more than once in the past. Even many of those who were mentally handicapped had been considered fit to plead on at least one previous occasion.

Comparisons of the unfit to plead with other mentally disordered offender groups can potentially shed light on why only a small proportion of mentally disordered defendants are found unfit to plead, but such comparisons need to be made cautiously as important biases will emerge depending on how the population is selected. There are in any case few systematic reports with which to compare, but a recent study of mentally disordered remand prisoners provides an interesting perspective (Dell et al., 1991). A direct comparison with this work, however, is limited by the fact that two of the three prisons studied were in inner London.

In general terms, the sample of mentally disordered remand prisoners described by Dell et al. was very similar to the unfit to plead defendants found in the current study. Prisoners thought by prison doctors to have been psychotic or mentally handicapped were older than other defendants, were often of non-Caucasian backgrounds, and frequently had both criminal and psychiatric histories in a way that was comparable with the unfit to plead population described here. The main difference between the two groups related to offence type. Criminal damage and public order offences accounted for about a quarter of the alleged offences in the remand group, whereas in the unfit to plead charges relating to personal violence were more frequent: Assaults were alleged to have been committed by 43% of the unfit to plead males and 52% of the unfit to plead females, compared with 31% of the mentally disordered Brixton Prison males (inner London), 12% of the Risley Prison males (Cheshire), 22% of the Holloway Prison females (inner London), and 32% of the Risley Prison females. Furthermore, compared with the remand sample, serious violence was more common among the unfit to plead who had been accused of assault-type crimes, accounting for about 40% of their violent offences compared with about 20% in the remand prisoners (though Dell et al. do not define "serious violence" and their criteria may have been different from those used in the current study).

The description by Walker and McCabe (1973) of mentally handicapped offenders who received hospital orders in 1963–1964 can also be used for comparison. Its findings were similar to the present study in that, like the mentally handicapped unfit to plead, the mentally handicapped offenders were younger than offenders who were mentally ill (with 28% under 20 years of age compared with 37% in the present study), many had criminal records, and sexual offences were over-represented in comparison with the mentally ill. The main difference in the unfit to plead was again related to offence type, with offences of personal violence uncommon in the mentally handicapped who received hospital orders, whereas over 30% of the mentally handicapped unfit to plead in the present study had been charged with either an assault or homicide.

Though it might be inferred from a comparison of the present study with the findings of Dell et al. and Walker and McCabe that the unfit to plead can in general be distinguished by their more violent and serious offences, it is still the case that only a minority of the unfit to plead were alleged to have committed serious offences, and about a third had been accused of offences rated as nuisance or of mild severity; similarly, violent and serious offences were not absent from the other populations. In terms of the remand sample, the difference between the groups is mainly accounted for by the large number of mentally disordered remand prisoners who are charged with public order type offences.

Of course, it may be the case that defendants found unfit to plead are more acutely unwell than other mentally disordered defendants, and those who have had previous contact with the criminal justice system may have been more unwell when found unfit to plead than they were on previous occasions. What evidence there is, however, does not support this view. One mentally handicapped man (case 035) in the current study, for example, had 11 previous convictions (mainly for theft-related offences though he did serve a three-year sentence for ABH), before being found unfit to plead to two charges of robbery in 1976. Conditionally discharged from hospital two years later (which meant that the Home Office continued to receive reports on his progress), he appeared in court on six further occasions with little apparent change in his mental state; he was convicted each time despite remaining technically unfit to plead to the original charge. He eventually served a six-month prison sentence before the Home Office finally lifted the restrictions that had been imposed on him by the CP(I)A.

Other accounts in the literature of mentally disordered offenders depict individuals with mental states that seem little different from that in the unfit to plead population described here. Haw and Cordess (1988), for instance, reported three cases of mute, mentally disordered defendants whose mental states were similar to that of many of the individuals in this study: A 37-year-old schizophrenic man charged with murder who was suspicious, had persecutory delusions and auditory hallucinations, and "refused to discuss the offence with anyone"; a 28-year-old schizophrenic woman charged with ABH and criminal damage who was uncooperative, suspicious and deluded, and refused to speak in court; and a 30-year-old schizophrenic man charged with GBH against his parents who refused to eat and drink while on remand and spoke only a few nonsensical words. In the first case the issue of fitness was not raised and the defendant was found guilty of manslaughter and given a hospital order, in the second case the prosecution dropped the charges, and in the third case the judge raised the issue of fitness but the prison doctor thought the defendant fit and the defence, reluctant to subject its client to a CP(I)A disposal, did not call medical evidence on fitness but did submit medical reports after a guilty verdict had been returned in order to secure a hospital order.

Dell et al. (1991) also found a relatively large number of mentally disordered defendants whose mental states did not appear to have been very different from that of many of the unfit to plead. For example, one remand prisoner they described was a man in his twenties who, while on holiday in the United Kingdom, suffered a schizophrenic breakdown and set fire to his address book in an Underground station for what were called delusional reasons. On remand he was acutely psychotic and violent. The prison doctor's medical report to the court stated that:

> He did not comprehend what was being said to him. He resorted to sudden, repeated and unprovoked attacks of violence to the staff responsible for his care. Many members of staff were required to restrain him from his violent fits. He went without food or drink offered to him. He appeared totally bewildered, confused and suspicious. He was incorrectly oriented in space and time, would give no account of himself and in fact did not converse but uttered unintelligible words as if conversing with imagined people.

Though technically this man must have been unfit to plead, no one seems to have raised the issue and he was found guilty of criminal damage. He received a conditional discharge and deportation order, but committed suicide in prison while awaiting removal from the country.

It is of interest that in the Dell et al. study, about 15% of medical remands to the two London prisons were for an assessment of fitness to plead (there were fewer to the prison outside London), yet in the four-and-a-half-month study period no one was actually found unfit. From these accounts it would appear that many more mentally disordered defendants could be found unfit to plead than is currently the case. Similarly it would seem that many of those found unfit to plead could have been dealt with in other ways: In some cases, the criminal charges could have been dropped and the individual offered psychiatric treatment either informally or under a civil section of the Mental Health Act, others could have been transferred to hospital for treatment while on remand with the aim of improving their mental states before trial, and others could simply have been dealt with definitively and fairly by the courts without the issue having been raised at all.

If there is so little to distinguish the unfit to plead from other mentally disordered defendants, why then is a select subgroup of mentally disordered defendants found unfit to plead? The answer would seem to lie not with the defendants themselves, but with those who are making the recommendations, and in the arbitrary, at times idiosyncratic ways in which they may reach their decisions. Indeed, a psychiatric recommendation of unfitness to plead often relates more to legal philosophy than it does to psychiatric considerations.

A good example of the arbitrary nature of the decision was the case of a schizophrenic man who in 1978 was found unfit to plead to a charge of murdering his baby nephew (case 064). He admitted the killing to the police and to various psychiatrists who examined him, saying that "the baby is always getting me into trouble so I hit it"; no one had any doubt that he was the perpetrator. The psychiatrist who recommended the unfitness finding wrote that the accused felt "he was being brainwashed and that people were out to lock him up . . . in my opinion he is clearly unfit to instruct solicitors or to plead to the present charges". When seen by a Mental Health Review Tribunal the following year, his solicitors and the tribunal both stated that he was fit to stand trial. The RMO, however, disagreed, and no recommendation was made to the Home Office. Subsequent tribunals and independent psychiatrists continued to state that the patient was fit, but it was not until his RMO was replaced in 1984 that, following a recommendation from his new RMO, he formally became fit to plead. He was eventually remitted for trial in 1986, more than eight years after the offence was committed, and he was found guilty of manslaughter. He remained psychotic throughout, and gave a variety of accounts of the offence; however, in the end his fitness to plead had little to do with him, but much to do with the doctor who was looking after him.

Many more examples such as this one could be given, but one case in particular stands out (case 062). This involved a 37-year-old mentally handicapped man who in 1978 was charged with stealing a bag of sweets and a tub of margarine from a shop, together worth about £2.00. The defence did not contest the facts of the case, but the psychiatrist who saw him for the defence wrote:

> On examination AF kept himself aloof from all conversation, keeping himself busy with sorting his old letters. He cannot concentrate in a manner long (sic) and his thinking jumps from one point to another. . . . In my view he 1) does understand the charges but says he simply forgot to pay for the items, 2) does not understand the difference between a plea of guilty and not guilty, 3) he is incapable of challenging jurors, 4) he is incapable of giving evidence and 5) he is incapable of instructing his solicitors and counsel due to mental handicap.

The prison doctor was convinced that AF was fit to plead, but was not called on to give evidence. AF was found unfit and sent to a mental handicap hospital, where the Home Office lifted restrictions immediately. The case is well summarised in a comment made by someone who became involved at a later stage: "As it was, a combination of apparently inexperienced solicitors and a forensically inexperienced consultant psychiatrist led to the defence pressing the issue of unfitness to plead, which resulted in the case being referred to the Crown Court with the present result".

The vagueness of the fitness criteria themselves is a contributing factor to the haphazard way in which some individuals can be found unfit to plead whereas other individuals with similar mental states are not. There is a tendency by many psychiatrists simply to report that a defendant meets one or more of the unfitness criteria, listing them parrot fashion, as described by Hess and Thomas (1963). But even when the grounds for the opinion are given, it is a simple matter to bend the criteria so that they fit the individual being assessed. For instance, in case 083 the prison doctor was able to argue that a mentally handicapped man who was planning to plead guilty to two charges of arson was unable to instruct his legal advisers because he was "confused about his motivation which engendered the offence"; in case 224 the doctor stated that though the accused knew what a plea of not guilty meant, "I doubt if he understands the true significance of these words"; in case 222 the defence psychiatrist reasoned that a schizophrenic man who wanted to plead not guilty to a charge of indecent assault could not instruct his solicitors because "by virtue of his delusions he can see no reason to plead guilty"; and in case 284 the defence psychiatrist said that a schizophrenic man who intended to plead guilty to a charge of wounding with intent in which the facts of the case were clear was unable to instruct counsel "because he does not recognise the validity of the court", and though he would be intellectually capable of following court proceedings, his abnormal beliefs meant that he could not do so "in any meaningful way".

In R v *Robertson* (1968) the Court of Appeal attempted to put a brake on the type of arguments advanced in the last two cases described when it stated that a paranoid mental state that interfered with the ability of a defendant to instruct his counsel "properly" was not sufficient for a finding of unfitness to plead. The reasoning would seem to be that it is up to a jury, not a doctor, to decide whether an explanation for an offence put forward by a defendant is reasonable or not. Regardless, many of the unfit to plead findings were based solely on the grounds that the accused wanted to offer a defence in which a criminal act was justified by psychotic reasoning.[1] The fact that this was allowed says much about the understanding of the law in relation to fitness to plead by both the medical and legal professions, and the ease with which the criteria can be manipulated.

The impreciseness of terms such as "comprehending court proceedings" and "properly instructing legal advisers" means that opinions about fitness to plead are largely subjective. There is a story, perhaps apocryphal, of a High Court judge who commented that if comprehension of court proceedings were a prerequisite for participation in a trial, then most of those in the courts, including members of the legal profession, would be considered unfit to plead. Whether this is true or not, it was observed that many patients who rapidly regained their fitness capacity after an unfitness finding did so simply because their RMOs, who were often not involved in the court decision, did not agree that their patients met the criteria in the first place. Because of these problems some writers have suggested that the criteria should be made the subject of statute (White, 1992), but it is unlikely that formalising the wording would serve to anchor the slippery structure.

The arbitrary nature of the process also relates to whether or not an attempt is made to secure psychiatric treatment before the unfitness finding is reached. Case 242 demonstrates well the relevance of this point. This case involved a schizophrenic man who in 1985 was found unfit to plead to two charges of wounding with intent, his victims being his brother and his brother's common-law-wife. Treated in hospital, he recovered his fitness rapidly, returned for trial seven months later, was found guilty, and was given a two-year probation order with a condition of treatment. Two years after this he was arrested again when he broke into a house and stole £200 worth of money and jewellery. On remand he was acutely psychotic, and both doctors who saw him considered him unfit to plead. On this second occasion, however, he was transferred to hospital for urgent treatment under section 48 of the Mental Health Act 1983, and within four months he had responded to treatment to the extent that his fitness to plead was no longer an issue; he was tried, found guilty, and received a hospital order without ever going down the unfitness route.

In this latter case there was no apparent reason why the approach taken in relation to his second offence could not have been taken at the time of his first trial. Indeed, in another case, where the accused had become acutely unwell in prison (case 250), the possibility of a section 48 transfer was suggested to the prison doctor, who decided instead that he would "try to arrange for the case to be listed as quickly as possible, and that [the defendant] will most probably be found unfit to plead. He has apparently started taking medication again, but is unlikely to improve quickly enough to become fit to plead". Why this prison doctor opted to pursue the unfitness option with such urgency when other, quicker routes to hospital treatment were open to him is unclear.

Whatever the attraction of an unfit to plead finding as opposed to pre-trial transfer to hospital for treatment, the fact is that only 5% of the unfit to plead population had been transferred to hospital for treatment *before* they were found unfit to plead (another 9% had at least some of their assessment in hospital as voluntary patients, some because they were already there at the time of their offences). It should be noted, however, that the apparent reluctance to transfer unsentenced prisoners to hospital is not limited to the unfit to plead; between 1976 and 1983, there were only about 20 such transfers a year,[2] though this has increased substantially in the 1990s.

If it is accepted that the process by which an individual is found unfit to plead is an arbitrary one, what lies at its root? Does it reflect an attempt by the state to detain some of its most marginal members, mentally disordered petty offenders, as some North American writers claim is the case in the United States and Canada (see Chapter 3)? Some support for this notion comes from the high proportion of individuals of no fixed abode (NFA) who make up the unfit to plead population (23%), many of whom had been charged with nuisance offences (it is interesting that about 40% of the remand sample described by Dell et al. (1991) were also of NFA). This type of explanation, however, loses some of its force when specific cases are considered.

For example, in a number of instances where individuals of NFA were charged with trivial offences it was often the prison doctor who pushed for the unfit to plead finding in an attempt to secure treatment for a mentally ill prisoner. Typically, the defendants were either acutely psychotic or extremely deteriorated schizophrenics who in the past had proved difficult or unresponsive patients, and whom catchment area hospitals were reluctant to have back, either informally or through the courts. The prison doctor, unhappy with this state of affairs, would then try to obtain an unfit to plead finding to take advantage of the Home Office's power to direct admission, thereby forcing a hospital to admit a patient it would not otherwise have accepted. At times, however, this ruse achieved more than the doctor expected, as the direction for admission was to a special hospital. Occasionally an explicit expression of this would surface in a doctor's report. For instance, in case 231 the prison doctor wrote "Should a jury return a verdict [of unfit to plead] then his future becomes the concern of the Home Secretary . . . it is patently obvious to me that it is the responsibility of the NHS to care for this man in the long term"; in another case (157) where a hospital bed was difficult to find " . . . he can therefore be regarded as unfit to plead in the event that there is no alternative disposal available"; and in another case (152) "I believe that it would be reasonable to make her unfit so that . . . the NHS will fulfil its obligations by giving her a bed".

These actions by prison doctors could be interpreted as examples of the state using psychiatry and psychiatric hospitals to remove from the community individuals whom the criminal justice system would otherwise have been powerless to detain, but it could also be argued that these doctors were simply trying to ensure, albeit in a heavy handed and in the end usually unproductive way, that individuals who they thought were in need of psychiatric care actually received that care.

Another type of case where it might be argued that the finding was used to obtain detention through a back door arose when the evidence against a defendant was weak, but the prosecution nevertheless believed the defendant was guilty. Case 015, a 75-year-old woman with dementia, was a good example of this. She was living in a nursing home in which a series of seven fires had broken out. Though she did not admit responsibility for the fires, she was linked to them by circumstantial evidence. She was transferred to a hospital geriatric ward and went to court from there, where she was found not guilty. Two weeks after her acquittal, however, a fire was set in a gents' toilet in the hospital where she was resident. She at first admitted setting this fire (and also the ones in the nursing home), but later retracted her confession. She was remanded in custody, where the prison doctor described her as " . . . an old lady who denies the charges . . . she is at times quite confused and is disoriented to time, place and person, this fluctuates so that she occasionally gives a good account of herself". On this second occasion, four months after she had been tried and acquitted of similar offences, she was found unfit to plead. The reluctance of the prosecution to risk a second acquittal is understandable, but it is also hard to imagine that this woman's mental state was very different at her second trial from what it was at her first court appearance a few months earlier. Proponents of natural justice would no doubt be concerned, but it should be pointed out that the result in this case was simply that she was returned to the hospital from which she came.

These types of situation, however, were not common. Because the option of a hospital order is more widely available to the courts of England and Wales than it is in North America, there are on the whole more straightforward ways of arranging for hospital detention, if that is the aim, than an unfit to plead finding, whatever the situation in relation to the equivalent finding in the United States and Canada.

A more likely explanation for the use of unfitness findings than quasi-sociological theories of state control is simply that the complexities of philosophical and legal issues can at times obscure the road down which both psychiatrists and lawyers are travelling. There were many individual examples of this, the most extreme being a seven page addendum to a psychiatric report (case 275), which addressed solely the issue of fitness to plead in the defendant, and in which the psychiatrist went on in great detail about the relevance of the "reification of fantasy". But perhaps more pertinent, because of its general acceptance, was the belief that it is just to detain someone as unfit to plead *only* if they are in fact the guilty party (at least in terms of having committed the act), and unjust to do so if there is any doubt about guilt; this has been crystallised with the introduction of a "trial of the facts" in the 1991 legislation. Witnesses told the Thomson Committee in Scotland, for instance, that the system there was working satisfactorily because (Scottish Home and Health Department and Crown Office, 1975, p.211):

> ... pleas of insanity in bar of trial were made only where the defence is satisfied that the accused person if tried would be convicted. This view is supported by the Crown Office practice never to indict unless there appears to be a sufficiency of evidence; in the vast majority of these cases the Crown would have little difficulty in proving the facts. Evidence from the Scottish Home and Health Department was that in practice it was rare for petitions to be received from mental patients detained following pleas in bar of trial which had as their ground a denial that the patient had committed the act charged; and that there was no recollection of any which raised doubts as to whether he had done so.

Similarly, in the present study there seemed little doubt that the unfit to plead defendant had committed the alleged offence in the vast majority of cases. But what purpose can an unfit to plead finding serve in cases where guilt is clear? It delays any eventual court appearance and definitive disposal, it complicates the management of psychiatric patients by involving the Home Office in cases where it would otherwise have had little interest, and it puts the patient at risk of indefinite hospital detention. More positive effects are less easy to find.

In the case of the mentally ill (as opposed to the mental handicapped) the belief that only those who committed the act in question should be found unfit to plead turns the concept of protection of the vulnerable defendant on its head. First, it tends to ignore questions related to *mens rea*.[3] Second, if guilt is so obvious, then there is no need to protect the accused from trial; he or she might as well be dealt with and be given a definitive disposal, which in the majority of cases would not involve the

Home Office in future management. From the descriptions of mentally disordered remand prisoners in Dell et al. (1991) and sentenced mentally disordered offenders in Walker and McCabe (1973), this is what must actually be happening in practice in the vast majority of cases; likewise, the fact that in Scotland pleas of insanity in bar of trial are made only where the defence believes that a conviction is highly likely means that those with similar mental states but whose guilt is in doubt will in fact be going to trial.

This is not to say that it is not unjust to detain an individual for a crime where there is real doubt about whether he or she was the guilty party, but it is precisely in these cases that an unfit to plead finding can work to the mentally disordered defendant's advantage. Rather than rushing these people into trial, the delay provided by an unfit to plead finding (or, better yet, a treatment period prior to the finding, as recommended by the Butler Committee) means that these individuals have an opportunity of receiving treatment and, if treatment is successful, will be more able to participate in their own defence, negating the need for a trial of the facts in their absence. Indeed, in cases where the issue is not one of whether the accused committed the act, but whether the necessary intention was present, the participation of the accused may be the only way to avoid a finding of guilt.

Support for this argument comes from the few not guilty findings that occurred in this study. The four cases described earlier (see p.78) undoubtedly benefited from treatment that followed the unfit to plead finding, and in the absence of more detail about their trials one can speculate that it was the improvement in their mental states that was responsible for their acquittals; all would undoubtedly have been found guilty at their initial trials if they had not been found unfit to plead instead. But the not guilty verdict returned in case 172 (LC) provides the clearest example of how an unfit to plead finding can protect the innocent:

> LC was a 39-year-old schizophrenic women who was found unfit to plead to a charge of arson in December 1982. The fire brigade, having been called to a fire at her flat, found her standing on a table, drunk and shouting obscenities out the kitchen window. She was forcibly removed from the flat, screaming "I'm going to burn the fucking place down". On remand she was floridly psychotic, but after the unfit to plead finding she received medication in hospital, and by April 1983 her RMO informed the Home Office that she had become fit to plead. She was tried in October of that year and found not guilty; the fire had been started by her 3-year-old

son who had been putting paper between the bars of an electric fire. It is likely that if she had been tried when acutely unwell she would have been found guilty; indeed, even a "trial of the facts" would probably have determined that she was responsible for the act.

The issue of detaining individuals as unfit to plead when their guilt is not clear has been confused by a failure to distinguish the mentally handicapped from the mentally ill, a confusion that has existed ever since Baron Alderson's misapplication of Hale in his formulation of the modern notion of fitness to plead in 1836 (see Chapter 2). The potential for a miscarriage of justice, such as occurred in the case of Valerie Hodgson, publicised by the Law Society (Law Society, 1991),[4] is most real in cases of mental handicap, though even here an adherence to PACE (Police and Criminal Evidence Act 1984) procedures for dealing with mentally handicapped suspects and diligence by defence lawyers should allow many of these trials to proceed, particularly when the details of the case are not in dispute. Do the mentally handicapped have any better understanding of the consequences of an unfit to plead finding than they do of court proceedings? Regardless, the fact that about a third of those with a primary diagnosis of mental handicap in this survey recovered their fitness to plead suggests that the initial finding may not have been altogether necessary in the first place.

Of course, the supposition that most unfit to plead findings are the result of misguided attempts by psychiatrists to apply legal philosophy in clinical situations is speculative. The only valid way to determine why some individuals are considered fit to plead whereas others who appear to be similar to them are not would be to compare the two groups in a prospective, interview-based study. Given the small number of unfit to plead findings that occur each year throughout the entire country, this would not be an easy study to carry out. In the absence of such research, one is left with the tentative conclusion that either many more individuals should be found unfit to plead each year than is currently the case, or that there are enough alternatives to an unfitness finding to make the procedure largely unnecessary.

THE EFFECTS OF THE FINDING

Regardless of whether or not more mentally disordered defendants should be found unfit to plead, it must still be asked whether the position of those who are actually found unfit to plead is better or worse than it would have been had their trials been allowed to go ahead.

The overall impression obtained from examining the files of those found unfit to plead was that the Home Office in general dealt with each case on its merits, and in a way similar to patients detained on ordinary hospital orders. It should be remembered that the bulk of the work carried out by C3 division in any case relates to the supervision of mentally disordered offenders. However, unlike most of the patients C3 deals with routinely, these individuals were *not* convicted offenders, and problems did arise on occasion from the confusion that this difference generated. The issues raised in the supervision of patients who may or may not have committed a crime, and whose condition may or may not have justified the imposition of restrictions on their discharge, carry with them their own special problems.

By the end of the survey period about a quarter of the sample were still detained in hospital under the provisions of the CP(I)A. It was clear, however, that detention in most of these "still detained" cases was justified in terms of their need for hospital treatment, with about two-thirds having made only limited improvement since their admissions (it is interesting that a woman who was described as "probably the most disturbed patient in Broadmoor at present, whether male or female" was sent there as unfit to plead, charged with an offence of moderate severity). Those still detained appeared to be a psychiatric rather than a criminal population: Over a third were actually in-patients at the time of their alleged offences, over a quarter were already long-term hospital patients, and nearly half had had a previous hospital admission that had lasted for more than a year.

Thus, many of the patients who were still detained in hospital under the provisions of the CP(I)A would probably have been in hospital anyway, even if they had never been admitted under the Act. The power that tribunals have had since 1983 to discharge CP(I)A patients if they are thought not to need compulsory treatment in hospital has further contributed to the likelihood that those patients who remain detained for extended periods under the provisions of the CP(I)A actually require hospital care.[5]

Just as important as the detail of the law itself, however, is the way in which the legislation is interpreted and acted on. For instance, the 1982 policy change, in which remission for trial became the preferred option when fitness capacity is regained, has had profound implications for those found unfit to plead. From that time, the patient's fitness status became more regularly enquired into by the Home Office but, more importantly, since 1982 more than 40% of those found unfit have had their cases heard in court, on average less than a year after the initial unfit to plead decision. Discharge through the courts also makes it less likely that a restriction order will remain with the patient unnecessarily.

It is worth noting, however, that about a fifth of those who remained detained in hospital under the provisions of the CP(I)A had recovered their fitness capacity but had not been tried. Though some of these individuals may eventually return to court, it could be argued that in the absence of an imminent trial continued detention of these patients in hospital, or the maintenance of a restriction order following their discharge, is not strictly justified. The rationale for the detention of these patients and their restricted discharge status rests with the requirement that it should be possible to produce them in court; if a trial is not going to take place, then this requirement becomes obsolete.

In addition, the amount of time spent in hospital prior to discharge from the conditions of the Act by a route other than court could be lengthy; even for those charged with nuisance or mild offences the mean period of hospital detention was 17.5 months. The relevance of this, however, is unclear. Though this length of time could be compared with that of alternative prison sentences, many of these individuals, particularly those charged with more serious offences, would probably have received some sort of hospital rather than prison disposal anyway, and there is no way of predicting how long they might have been detained in hospital under the relevant provisions of the Mental Health Act.

The most serious concern in relation to an unfitness finding (possible life detention in hospital) did not emerge in practice as a substantial risk, though this must be said with reservation. There is an unknown number of patients detained in the hospital system who were found unfit to plead before 1976, and though many will still need hospital treatment, it only requires a small number of "unjustifiable" cases before the numbers add up to a significant collection of people. Even so, this is still very unlike the situation in the United States pre-1972 when, as in England and Wales today, the length of detention following an incompetent to stand trial finding was not subject to statutory limitations; it was found there that incompetent patients were frequently spending the rest of their lives in hospital (see Chapter 3). This difference between England and Wales and the United States probably relates to two factors: First, in the former a single government department, accustomed to monitoring mentally disordered offenders, has responsibility for the supervision of unfitness cases, and second, Mental Health Review Tribunals are able to discharge patients who are inappropriately detained.

The more common type of problem associated with an unfit to plead finding had less to do with issues of detention *per se*, and more to do with the constraints placed on RMOs in the treatment and rehabilitation of their patients. Even in cases where public safety was not an issue, the Home Office had to be consulted on all decisions relating to the relaxation of supervision, despite the fact that its involvement in these cases arose not from concerns about a patient's dangerousness, but as an automatic consequence of the patient's inability to plead and the legalistic requirement of ensuring that a return to court could take place if necessary. Once restrictions were in place, there was sometimes a reluctance by the Home Office to remove them, particularly when the alleged offence was serious or reports on the patient were worrying; the situation could also arise in a patient who did not represent a great risk to the public, but about whom the Home Office felt uncomfortable in granting an absolute discharge because of persistent management problems in relation to relapses of his or her mental illness, even if it did not maintain an active involvement in the case. For example:

> In case 004 a schizophrenic man was found unfit to plead in October 1976 to a charge of stealing a jacket worth £10. In September 1977 he was granted a conditional discharge, but his restriction order was not lifted because he had a history of defaulting on his medication. He remained well in the community for four years, but then refused his medication and became psychotic. Recall was considered, but as he was not regarded as dangerous it did not take place; instead, he was admitted under a civil section of the Mental Health Act 1959. Over the next three years his management was not straightforward; he refused medication, he was paranoid and he was aggressive, but he was never seen as dangerous. Finally, in October 1985, nine years after the unfit to plead finding, he was granted an absolute discharge when it became clear that he could "quite well be left to society's normal mechanisms".

The situation regarding dangerousness and patient containment, however, could be more problematic. In case 204, the RMO of a mentally handicapped patient wrote to the Home Office, clearly frustrated by what he saw as Home Office delay in granting leave, "I feel I must again write to ask for permission for this patient to go on outings . . . the situation is that she is the only patient on a ward of 18 who is not leaving the hospital at all and this is making her demoralised". This was a patient who had been charged with arson and whose behaviour in hospital had at times been worrying, and the Home Office had justifiable concerns about her; however, she had in fact recovered her fitness to plead and was waiting to return to court for trial. Four months after the

RMO had written to the Home Office, the patient returned to court where her case was adjourned for two months; she went back to hospital, no longer under the conditions of the CP(I)A, and the RMO was able to allow her to go on as many outings as he pleased. She was eventually tried, found guilty, and was given a hospital order without restrictions.

INHERENT PROBLEMS

Though the risk of possible life detention in hospital on the basis of allegations rather than proven offences appears to diminish in importance when the perspective is changed from theory to practice, there are a number of other issues that do arise from the periodic friction between legal and psychiatric priorities. Difficulties associated with findings of unfitness to plead have their origins in two sources: Those that are caused by problems ingrained in the legislation, and those that are intrinsic to the concept of fitness to plead itself. Some of these have already been discussed—in particular the arbitrary nature of the criteria and their application, the lack of any provision to ensure that treatment is offered to the mentally ill before a finding, the inflexibility of disposal and confusion about what is supposed to be achieved by the finding. Other inherent problems are described below, together with illustrative cases.

1. The status of the patient does not change once fitness to plead is recovered.   On recovery of fitness, there is no obligation for the Home Secretary to remit the patient for trial, nor is he required to lift the patient's discharge restrictions. Even if the Home Secretary decides to remit, the prosecution may not wish to proceed with the case. The court itself is not a party to any of these decisions. This means that the accused patient, unlike any other individual charged with a crime, is not assured of an opportunity to prove his or her innocence, and if guilty, of having a judge decide the sentence:

> In case 271, a mentally handicapped 21-year-old man was accused of indecently assaulting his 5-year-old stepsister. There were physical signs to suggest that the girl had been abused, but the only evidence against the defendant was a statement he made at the police station; otherwise he consistently denied the offence. The patient's RMO, in fact, came to believe that another member of the family might have been responsible. After nine months in hospital his RMO said that he had become fit to plead, and the Home

Office consulted with the Crown Prosecution Service (CPS) about the possibility of mounting a trial. The CPS said that though witnesses were available and evidence could be presented, it would not be in the public interest to proceed. The patient's solicitors, however, believed that the evidence against their client was extremely weak, and they persisted in their view that the case should be heard. The Home Office again contacted the CPS, implying strongly that it felt a trial should go ahead (the Home Office, of course, has no authority to insist that the CPS act), but because of problems inherent in their case the CPS would not change its decision; the patient's solicitors considered seeking judicial review. The situation was finally resolved when the Home Office agreed to lift the restriction order. If the charges against the patient had been more serious, however, it is unlikely that the Home Office would have felt able to take this course, and the patient would have remained a restriction order patient based on an alleged offence that he did not have the opportunity to refute.

2. The criteria by which an individual is found unfit to plead are not the same as those that determine whether or not treatment in hospital is appropriate. This means that when a patient is ready to be discharged from hospital he is still liable for re-arrest on the original charge by the police; if still unfit to plead, this could theoretically result in a cycle of arrest, an unfitness to plead finding, hospital detention, discharge, re-arrest, and so on. In practice, when discharge was being considered and fitness had not been recovered, the Home Office usually confirmed with the prosecuting authorities that they did not plan to proceed against the patient, but problems could arise if they insisted on pursuing the case. Two examples where the cycle nearly started are:

> In case 147 a mentally handicapped man was found unfit to plead in 1981 to charges of arson and burglary. By 1983 he was thought ready for discharge, but when the Assistant Chief Constable was contacted he wrote that though he accepted the patient remained unfit to plead, "he is in my opinion a dangerous man ... and I cannot see my way clear to abandoning our intention to take proceedings against him at this stage". Fortunately a compromise was eventually reached whereby a test period in the community was agreed.

> In case 230, a mentally handicapped man was found unfit to plead in November 1984 to charges of arson. He was sent to

a special hospital by direction because, though initially refused admission, local units had also refused to accept him. In June 1985, about eight months after the finding and while still considered unfit to plead, a Mental Health Review Tribunal ordered his conditional discharge. The police were very concerned about "the likely effect that the release of [the patient] would have both on [the patient] himself and on the community in general", and concluded that "the best course of action" would be to bring him back before the court. The situation was resolved when his RMO stated that the patient had become fit to plead; he was tried, found guilty, and received a guardianship order.

3. After a finding of unfitness to plead, the RMO becomes the arbiter of whether fitness is regained. This is not strictly necessary by law as the CP(I)A states only that the Secretary of State should consult with the responsible medical officer, but in practice it was only once the RMO said that the patient had become fit that the Home Office would take matters further. Though Mental Health Review Tribunals can comment on fitness to plead, they have no authority to determine whether fitness has been regained. Case 064, which has already been described (see p.89), is a good example of how an RMO with idiosyncratic views on what constitutes fitness to plead can insist that a patient remains unfit despite many opinions to the contrary. In that case there was little doubt that the patient had committed the offence, but where the facts are less clear such a stance by an RMO may have profound implications for natural justice.

4. The question of whether it is possible for a trial to go ahead is not pursued until the patient is said to have recovered fitness to plead.
This means that a patient can be detained for many years on the basis that if fitness is recovered, remission for trial will follow. The possibility of a trial, however, may have been nonexistent from early on in the patient's detention:

Case 224 involved a mentally handicapped man accused of indecently assaulting a 3-year-old girl in 1984. In 1987 he was said by his RMO to have become fit to plead. Because the victim was by then 6 years old, and because much of the evidence depended on the man's own confession at the time, the police said they would not (and indeed could not) bring him back to trial. Clearly a trial had not been possible for some time, but this was not acknowledged until he was declared fit to plead. It was fortuitous that in this case his fitness was recovered after only 3 years of detention; it could have occurred much later, as it has for other patients.

Given these various difficulties, it is perhaps not surprising that both lawyers and psychiatrists are often reluctant to recommend that the issue of fitness to plead should even be considered. Not infrequently, cases are simply dealt with by the courts and defendants are either acquitted or found guilty and sentenced without the issue having been raised at all.

REFORM

The Butler Committee's report on mentally abnormal offenders (Home Office & DHSS, 1975) provided a thorough review of the law in relation to fitness to plead in England and Wales; it also contained a number of recommendations for reform. Some of its suggestions for change were technical in nature, such as replacing the term "fitness to plead" with "under disability in relation to trial" as the Committee felt that the former was both inaccurate and misleading. Other suggestions were more in the nature of fine-tuning than radical reform, such as the recommendation that the *agreed* evidence of two doctors should be required before a finding could be reached. Also in the category of fine-tuning was the Committee's proposal that the criteria for unfitness should be altered so that the ability to challenge a juror would no longer be included, and that two new criteria, the ability to plead with understanding to the indictment, and the ability to give adequate instructions to legal advisers, would be added (though in practice both were already in use). Given the tendency of doctors and lawyers to bend the criteria to fit the circumstances, however, it is not clear how much of an impact this type of alteration might have.

However, the Committee also made a number of other proposals that, taken together, had the potential to bring about much more substantial change. The Committee recommended that:

- The trial judge should decide on the question of disability except in cases where the medical evidence was disputed *and* the defence requested that the matter should be decided by a jury.
- If recovery was likely, the judge could adjourn the proceedings for up to six months before the issue was determined.

- If the accused remained under disability at the end of the adjourned period (and immediately where recovery was unlikely, such as in cases of severe subnormality), a trial of the facts would take place that would include an examination of whether the defendant had the necessary mental state at the time of the offence.

- If the accused was found under disability and was found "guilty" by a trial of the facts (the verdict would not in fact be one of guilt but of "under disability"), the court would have some discretion regarding disposal. Hospital and guardianship orders were included among the court's options, but probation, supervision, and community service orders were not, as they would render the defendant liable to a return to court in the event of default. A prison sentence was also not included in the list of possible disposals.

- Magistrates' courts would also be able to determine the issue, but at the same time the Committee did not feel that this should be encouraged in minor cases.

Based on the findings of the present study, the Butler recommendation calling for an adjournment of proceedings would seem to be a sensible one, though the six-month time limit may be unduly short. Of the 135 patients who were said to have recovered their fitness capacity, half had done so within four months and 60% within six; of the 76 who returned for trial, three-quarters had recovered their fitness by six months. About 30% of the sample, therefore (60% of the 49% who were said to have recovered fitness)[6] would have avoided an unfitness finding if a six-month treatment period had been in force, though the true figure is probably higher, given the delay by RMOs in informing the Home Office about recovery. Though it was difficult to judge how often appropriate medication was initiated pre-trial, 80% of the population had their full assessments in prison, where circumstances might be thought less conducive to an improvement in mental state. A statutory treatment period, therefore, would seem to have the potential of drastically reducing the number of unfitness findings.

Counterbalancing the effect of this proposed reform, however, was the possible increase in findings that might follow from allowing the issue to be determined in magistrates' courts. Similarly, the expanded options for disposal might tempt some lawyers to take advantage of the unfitness option to protect their clients from prison. Perhaps the Committee hoped that inappropriate findings would be short-circuited by having the question decided by a judge in the majority of cases.

In any event, the Butler recommendations were never implemented, though the Criminal Procedure (Insanity and Unfitness to Plead) Act 1991 did follow up a number of them. Because this legislation was initiated as a private member's bill, it had to be "brief, straightforward and uncontentious" (White, 1992). Its two major changes, a trial of the facts and more flexible disposal options, have already been described (see p.25).[7] In addition, the Act requires that the evidence of two or more doctors should be heard before a finding can be reached (though interestingly it does not demand *agreement* between the doctors as suggested by Butler), and it allows remission directly from hospital to court, thus removing an anomaly of the CP(I)A 1964 in which remission for trial had to be preceded by a return to prison.

Though the shadow of the Butler recommendations can be seen in the 1991 Act, the substance of the Act differs from Butler in significant ways. First, as already mentioned, the *agreed* evidence of two doctors in respect of a patient's fitness is not required. In the current study, as has already been described, disagreement between doctors about fitness was not infrequent, although those responsible for the Act may have believed that disagreement is no bad thing given that it is a jury, and not psychiatrists, who decide the issue. Second, there is no provision in the Act for an adjournment before the decision is reached. It might be argued, however, that more energetic pre-trial treatment of mentally disordered defendants (and by implication those who are unfit to plead), and greater use of hospital transfers under the Mental Health Act 1983, as advocated in other concurrent reviews (for instance, in the recent Home Office/Department of Health *Review of services for mentally disordered offenders*; Department of Health/Home Office, 1991). And third, the trial of the facts as outlined in the Act is limited to a consideration of whether the accused committed the act or made the omission charged, with no consideration given to intent, or *mens rea*. This last point may create difficulties in offences such as blackmail, kidnapping or, as pointed out by White (1992), shoplifting, where it is not the act but the intention that is most important.

It is interesting that neither the Butler Committee nor the 1991 Act place any emphasis on the desirability of bringing the unfit to plead patient back to trial. Indeed, in the 1991 Act the possibilities for doing so have been reduced as remission can now only occur for those patients who receive hospital orders *with* restrictions on discharge. For the Butler Committee, this attitude may have arisen because it believed (wrongly) that if recovery of fitness had not taken place by the end of the six-month adjournment period then it was unlikely to occur; the framers of the 1991 Act, on the other hand, may have reasoned that remission is best pursued only in more serious cases that would anyway attract a restriction order. Both the Butler Committee report and the explanatory notes to the 1991 Act stress that, despite a positive outcome of a trial of facts, an unfitness finding is not equivalent to a finding of guilt. However, the Butler Committee did acknowledge that the verdict was in essence "one of guilty in all but name" (p.150), and an argument can therefore be made that those found unfit to plead should have more scope for their cases to be heard in court in the event of recovery.

It has already been mentioned that the Butler Committee was by and large content with the criteria for unfitness themselves, commenting that most observers thought they worked well; the 1991 Act makes no mention of the criteria at all. Neither recognised the problems inherent in applying criteria originally developed for individuals of limited cognitive ability to those whose reasoning is distorted by mental disorder, and the arbitrary and idiosyncratic way in which decisions about fitness are finally reached. Although some commentators have suggested that the criteria should be tightened through legislation (White, 1992), it has also been argued more radically that the criteria should be abolished altogether, to be replaced by a decision made by the judge about whether a defendant's mental state is such that it would preclude a fair trial (Grubin, 1993). This latter suggestion would place fitness to plead on a par with how decisions are made in the context of the Police and Criminal Evidence Act 1984 (PACE) in relation to whether particular pieces of evidence, or confessions, should be allowed. Here, no specific criteria are stated,[8] and case law has determined that judges should have maximum flexibility: In R v *Samuel* (1987), for example, Hodgson J. commented "It is undesirable to attempt any general guidance as to the way in which a judge's discretion under section 78 or his inherent powers should be exercised. Circumstances vary infinitely", and in R v *Jelen and Katz* (1990), Auld J. stated "This is not an apt field for hard case law and well-founded distinction between cases". Similar principles could easily be applied to decisions about an individual's fitness to plead.

Now that a hospital order with restrictions on discharge is no longer a mandatory outcome, the most likely effect of the 1991 Act will be a gradual increase in the number of individuals found unfit to plead. If this turns out to be the case, the change may not be for the better. A procedure that evolved to ensure that mentally disordered defendants would not be tried unfairly may have developed into one that causes them to be convicted at a trial of facts that takes place in their absence, which takes no account of whether there was any intention to commit a crime, and which may prevent them from having a definitive trial during which they are both present and competent.

NOTES

1. Another example of this was a psychotic man who admitted that he had not paid a taxi fare, but insisted that he had committed no crime because he owned the taxi (case 202).

2. These figures were calculated by Dr Graham Robertson of the Institute of Psychiatry from *Supplemental reports to the criminal statistics* for these years.

3. The Criminal Procedure (Insanity and Unfitness to Plead) Act 1991 explicitly excludes considerations of intention.

4. According to the Law Society's account, Hodgson was a mentally handicapped woman who lived with her elderly father. One morning she found him dead on the floor, stabbed in the chest. She confessed to the crime, was found unfit to plead, and was sent to a mental handicap hospital. More than a year later, however, it transpired that her nephew was responsible for the murder. If the actual offender had not been apprehended, Hodgson could have been detained for life without trial, assumed to have committed a crime of which she was innocent. Though the Law Society's rendering of the case was greatly simplified and not altogether accurate, its implications remain unchanged. The case was among those reviewed in this study, but because she has been identified it is not possible to discuss its details without breaching confidentiality.

5. Remaining unfit to plead is not a bar to hospital discharge, and more than half of those unfit to plead patients who were discharged by tribunals had not regained their fitness capacity.

6. Excluding the 18 special warrant patients (see p.67)

7. As mentioned in Chapter 2, the disposal options in the 1991 Act are: a hospital order with or without restrictions on discharge, a guardianship order, a supervision and treatment order, and an absolute discharge, though when the charge is murder a hospital order with restrictions is mandatory.

8. PACE states that: "In any proceedings the court may refuse to allow evidence . . . [if] having regard to all the circumstances in which the evidence was obtained, the admission of the evidence would have such an adverse effect on the fairness of the proceedings that the court ought not to admit it".

CHAPTER SEVEN

Conclusion and recommendations

The number of defendants found unfit to plead in England and Wales has been declining steadily for about 70 years, and at present only a very few individuals are found unfit to plead each year. The concept of fitness to plead, however, is intimately associated with the theoretical underpinnings of British law. Although it is unlikely ever to be abandoned completely, attempts to mould the concept to adapt it to changing legal and psychiatric thinking have not on the whole been successful. Indeed, it is ironic that a concept that evolved to protect vulnerable defendants from the rigours of an unfair trial may now have the unintended consequence of entrapping them in a nether world somewhere between the criminal justice and mental health systems. Patients who recover their fitness to plead are pointed not towards discharge and rehabilitation, but towards a court appearance and formal sentencing.

Recent legislative reform intended to make the consequences of being found unfit to plead both more rational and humane may revitalise the concept. It may very well result in an increased use of the finding. But is this something that should be encouraged? Instead of expansion, perhaps the time has come to trim the concept back to its essential component, the notion of a fair trial; at the same time, the opportunity could be taken to abandon the 19th-century understanding of what actually constitutes a psychiatric impediment to a fair trial.

Amidst the legal argument that has grown abundantly around the issue of what fitness to plead means, one can lose sight of those mentally disordered defendants who are affected by it. For most, the issue of a fair trial is irrelevant. There is frequently little question that they carried out the relevant act, and the defence often has no intention of contesting the facts of the case. For the defendants, what matters is that they should receive proper treatment, in an appropriate setting, and as rapidly as possible; in addition, society needs to be protected from the minority of them who may be dangerous. In addition, however, there is also the need to protect them from criminal stigmatisation in cases where the intent to offend was lacking. Unfitness to plead, in the form of the CP(I)A 1964, and the Criminal Procedure (Insanity and Unfitness to Plead) Act 1991 are cumbersome ways to meet these objectives. Other legislation targeted more specifically at the mentally disordered, in particular the 1959 and 1983 Mental Health Acts, has proved to be a much more effective way of achieving these goals. This should hardly be surprising: Being unfit to plead is not a psychiatric diagnosis, it is a legal concept, and it has little meaning in terms of treatment, prognosis, or management.

The goal should be to restrict the use of unfitness to plead to appropriate cases, and to discourage its use otherwise. Because it is concerned with the issue of a fair trial, it should be limited to situations where there is doubt about the facts or intent, in other words, to cases where there is actually something to be tried in court. Where these issues are clear, the defendant needs to be protected not from the trial process, but from those who want to find him unfit to plead.

In addition to restricting the issue of fitness to plead in this way, there should also be an underlying assumption that the consideration of fitness to plead is a last resort; a trial in the presence of a competent defendant is to be preferred to a "trial of facts" in a defendant's absence. Factors such as the seriousness of the charge, the complexity of the evidence in the case, and the nature of the mental disorder will all have a bearing on this decision, that is, whether in any particular case an individual's mental state is such that a subsequent conviction would be unsafe.

If the concept were to be contained within these confines, it is likely that cases in which fitness to plead needed to be considered would be primarily of two types. The first would relate to those defendants who are psychiatrically very unwell and who have been accused of serious offences: floridly psychotic individuals who do not respond to treatment in hospital within a reasonable period of time, or patients with severe mental handicap who cannot be assisted through the trial process. Prosecuting authorities might be reluctant to let cases drop in view of the seriousness of the charges, but given doubts about guilt, it would be inappropriate to detain these patients long-term on a pre-trial section of the Mental Health Act 1983. The second type of case will involve individuals, sometimes psychotic, sometimes personality disordered, sometimes mentally handicapped, in whom guilt is unclear but who will nevertheless want to plead guilty for reasons related to their mental disorders. The type or degree of mental disorder in these individuals may not allow for treatment under the Mental Health Act 1983, but a mechanism is necessary to prevent them from falsely incriminating themselves. It is worth noting that at present the issue of fitness to plead is rarely raised in the latter type of situation, and when it is, legal interpretation about what it means to "properly" instruct legal advisers makes a positive finding problematic (cf. R v *Robertson*, 1968).

In summary then, it is argued that fitness to plead should be more firmly focused on the issue of a fair trial in cases where guilt is in doubt. It should be turned to as a last resort, when the provisions of the Mental Health Act 1983 have been exhausted or when they can not be applied. The following recommendations are made with these basic principles in mind:

1. The issue of fitness to plead should be decided in all cases by a judge, rather than by a jury as at present.[1] The judge should make his decision in light of the facts of the case and when guilt is unclear, depending on whether he believes that a conviction would be unsafe because of mental disorder in the defendant. The judge should be satisfied that there are no alternative pre-trial treatment options available within the Mental Health Act 1983. No formal criteria for fitness to plead would need to be met, with the decision being taken in a similar way to decisions about the admissibility of evidence and confessions as outlined in the Police and Criminal Evidence Act 1984 (PACE).

2. In cases of mental illness, once the issue of fitness to plead is raised but before a finding is reached, there should be a mandatory period of treatment in hospital, lasting a maximum of six months. In cases of mental handicap, such a pre-finding treatment period would be optional.

3. If a defendant is found unfit to plead, there should be a trial of the facts of the case. This would also take into account the intent, or *mens rea*, of the defendant as outlined in the Butler Committee report. A "guilty" verdict would be recorded as "a finding of unfit to plead *and* proven"; a "not guilty" finding would be recorded as a plain acquittal.

4. Disposal options should be those currently outlined in the Criminal Procedure (Insanity and Unfitness to Plead) Act 1991.

5. In cases of "unfit to plead *and* proven", the judge should set a time period over which, if the patient's mental state improved and he or she contested the verdict, a trial could still be held; a restriction order would not be necessary for a future trial to take place. Beyond this time limit no appeal would be allowed. If a hospitalised patient contested disposal, a Mental Health Review Tribunal should have the power to consider the question and to alter the disposal as appropriate.

6. Only the patient can challenge the verdict or disposal, as outlined in recommendation 5.

It should be emphasised that these recommendations are intended as general guidelines relating primarily to psychiatric issues of fitness to plead; more detailed, legally oriented aspects of the finding are beyond the scope of this work.

The concept of fitness to plead is firmly rooted in the soil of legal tradition, but in recent years it has been more a theoretical component of the trial process than one that has been applied to any great extent. It is meant to protect the mentally disordered defendant from the rigours of the court, but in its current formulation it tends to be applied to the wrong individuals in the wrong circumstances. Reformulated, however, it could offer valuable protection to the most vulnerable of mentally disordered defendants.

NOTE

1. As the Butler Committee pointed out, juries are not usually involved in decisions about whether a trial should proceed or whether an untried defendant should be sent to hospital.

APPENDIX

Data collection schedule

File year: 19 ___

ID number   _____

Date of birth   _____

Date of arrest   _____

Date of decision   _____

Sex   ____
  (1 male; 2 fem)

Ethnic origin   ____
  (1 Cauc; 2 Afro; 3 Car; 4 Ind sub; 5 Asia; 6 Other)

Place of birth   ____
  (1 UK; 2 Afro; 3 Car; 4 Ind sub; 5 Asia; 6 Ire; 7 Eur; 8 Other)

Occupation

Worked in last year   _____
(1 no; 2 yes)

Criminal Record [record CRO with disposals; continue over]   _____
(0 none; 1 nonviolent only; 2 any violent)

Psychiatric History (continue over)   _____
[account; record number admissions, admissions on sections,
age first contact, age first admission, diagnoses, history of
brain damage]

In-patient at offence   _____
(1 no; 2 yes)
Psychiatric care at time of offence   _____
(1 no; 2 yes)
If not in care, time out of care (mths)   _____
Defaulted   _____
(1 no; 2 yes)

IQ   _____
NFA   _____
(1 no; 2 yes)

Charge [offence; record details]:

theft/fraud _____
damage to property _____
weapon _____
violence _____
sex offence _____
arson _____
assault police _____
homicide _____
other _____

Severity   _____
(1 nuisance; 2 mild; 3 moderate; 4 severe)

Disorder at time of offence   _____
(0 none; 1 ment ill; 2 pers dis; 3 ment hand; 4 addict)

Change in mental state since offence   _____
  (1 no; 2 yes)

"Under disability" raised by   _____
  (1 prosecution; 2 defence; 3 judge)

"Under disability" raised when   _____
  (1 pre-trial; 2 start of trial; 3 after pros case)

Place of assessment   _____
  (1 no: 2 yes)

                                          prison _____
                              hosp op (on bail) _____
                              hosp in-patient _____
                                   any section _____

Treatment before finding [record]
  (1 no; 2 yes)

                                          prison _____
                                   out-patient _____
                                    in-patient _____
                                    on section _____

Admits charge   _____
  (1 denies; 2 admits; 3 varies; 4 no comment)

BASIS OF DECISION

Psychiatrist [name, hospital]

Fit   _____
  (1 no; 2 yes; 3 no comment)

Criteria

                              instruct counsel _____
                              challenge juror _____
                              understand plea _____
                          understand evidence _____
                             comp proceedings _____
                                         other _____

Opinion [record details of mental state,
  reason for unfitness] date   _____

Psychiatrist: [name, hospital]

Fit   _____
  (1 no; 2 yes; 3 no comment)

Criteria

                                      instruct counsel _____
                                       challenge juror _____
                                       understand plea _____
                                   understand evidence _____
                                     comp proceedings _____
                                                 other _____

Opinion [record details of mental state,
  reason for unfitness] date   _____

Conflict   _____
  (1 no; 2 yes)

Hospital sent to:

Date arrived in hospital   _____

Type of hospital   _____
  (1 local; 2 med sec; 3 special; 4 private)

OUTCOME
Recovers fitness   _____
  (1 no; 2 yes)
Date recovers fitness   _____

Trial   _____
  (1 no; 2 yes)

If trial:
Date   _____

Verdict   ———
 (1 not guilty; 2 guilty; 3 charges dropped, etc.)
Sentence   ———
 (1 Noncust; 2 prison; 3 hosp order, not sh; 4 hosp order, sh)
Restriction order   ———
 (1 no; 2 yes)
Length of prison sentence (mths)   ————

If not trial:
Outcome   ———
 (1 same hosp; 2 transfer hosp; 3 cond disc; 4 abs disc;
  5 rest lift; 6 death; 7 other)
Date of hospital discharge   ————————————
Reason for discharge without trial:

Primary diagnosis   ———
Secondary diagnosis (i)   ———
Secondary diagnosis (ii)   ———
 (1 schizophrenia; 2 depression; 3 mania; 4 alcohol or drug
  psychosis; 5 other psychosis; 6 mental handicap; 7 neurotic
  disorder; 8 personality disorder; 9 brain damage; 10 none;
  11 serious diag. difficulties)

Record progress (over)

References

Arvanites, T. M. (1989). The differential impact of deinstitutionalization on white and nonwhite defendants found incompetent to stand trial. *Bulletin of the American Academy of Psychiatry and the Law, 17,* 311–320.

Chiswick, D. (1978). Insanity in bar of trial in Scotland: A state hospital study. *British Journal of Psychiatry, 132,* 598–601.

Chiswick, D. (1990a). Fitness to stand trial and plead, mutism and deafness. In R. Bluglass & P. Bowden (Eds.), *Principles and practice of forensic psychiatry.* London: Churchill Livingstone.

Chiswick, D. (1990b). Reprosecution of patients found unfit to plead: A report of anomalies in procedure in Scotland. Psychiatric Bulletin, 14, 208–210.

"Comment". (1951). Lunacy and idiocy - the old law and its incubus. *University of Chicago Law Review, 18,* 361–368.

Cooke, G., Johnston, N., & Pogany, E. (1973). Factors affecting referral to determine competency to stand trial. *American Journal of Psychiatry, 130,* 870–875.

Criminal Statistics for England and Wales. (1982). London: HMSO.

Cuneo, D. J., Brelje, T. B., Randolph, J. J., & Taliana, L. E. (1982). Seriousness of charge and length of hospitalization for the unfit defendant. *Journal of Psychiatry and Law, 10,* 163–171.

Dean, M. (1960). Fitness to plead. *Criminal Law Review,* 79–86.

Dell, S., Grounds, A., James, K., & Robertson, G. (1991). *Mentally disordered remanded prisoners.* Unpublished report to the Home Office.

Department of Health/Home Office. (1991). *Review of health and social services for mentally disordered offenders and others requiring similar services: Report of the prison advisory group.* London: HMSO.

Emmins, C. (1986). Unfitness to plead: Thoughts prompted by Glenn Pearson's case. *Criminal Law Review,* 604–618.

Furneaux, R. (1960). *Guenther Podola.* London: Stevens & Sons.

Geller, J. L., & Lister, E. D. (1978). The process of criminal commitment for pretrial psychiatric examination: An evaluation. *American Journal of Psychiatry, 135,* 53–60.

Golding, S. L., Roesch, R., & Schreiber, J. (1984). Assessment and conceptualization of competency to stand trial: Preliminary data on the Interdisciplinary Fitness Interview. *Law and Human Behavior, 8,* 321–334.

Golding, S. L., & Roesch, R. (1988). Competency for abjudication: An international analysis. In D. N. Weisstub (Ed.), *Law and mental health: International perspectives,* (Vol. 4). Oxford: Pergamon Press.

Gostin, L. (1986). *Mental health services - law and practice.* London: Shaw and Sons, Ltd.

Griffiths, A. (1884). *The Chronicles of Newgate.* London: Chapman and Hall, Ltd.

Grubin, D. (1991a). Unfit to plead in England and Wales, 1976–1988: A survey. *British Journal of Psychiatry, 158,* 540–548.

Grubin, D. (1991b). Regaining fitness: Patients found unfit to plead who return for trial. *Journal of Forensic Psychiatry, 2,* 139–151.

Grubin, D. H. (1991c). Unfit to plead, unfit for discharge: Patients found unfit to plead who are still in hospital. *Criminal Behaviour and Mental Health, 1,* 282–294.

Grubin, D. (1993). What constitutes fitness to plead? *Criminal Law Review,* 748–758.

Hale, Sir M. (1971). *The history of the pleas of the Crown* (Vols. i & ii). London: Professional Books.

Harding, T. (1992). A comparative survey of medico-legal systems. In J. Gunn & P. J. Taylor (Eds.), *Forensic psychiatry: Clinical, legal and ethical issues.* London: Butterworth-Heinemann.

Haw, C. M., & Cordess, C. C. (1988). Mutism and the problem of the mute defendant. *Medicine, Science and the Law, 28,* 157–164.

Hess, J. H., & Thomas, H. E. (1963). Incompetency to stand trial: Procedures, results, and problems. *American Journal of Psychiatry, 119,* 713–720.

Hibbert, C. (1963). *The roots of evil.* London: Weidenfeld & Nicolson.

Holdsworth, Sir W. S. (1922). *A history of English law* (Vol. i, 3rd ed.). London: Methuen.

Home Department. (1963). *Third Report of the Criminal Law Revision Committee: Criminal Procedure (Insanity),* cmnd. 2149. London: HMSO.

Home Office & DHSS. (1975). *Report of the Committee on Mentally Abnormal Offenders* (The Butler Report), cmnd. 6244. London: HMSO.

Kunjukrishnan, R. (1979). Ten-year survey of pretrial examinations in Saskatchewan. *Canadian Journal of Psychiatry, 24,* 683–689.

Lamb, H. R. (1987). Incompetency to stand trial. *Archives of General Psychiatry, 44,* 754–758.

Larkin, E. P., & Collins, P. J. (1989). Fitness to plead and psychiatric reports. *Medicine, Science and the Law, 29,* 26–32.

Law Society. (1991). *Criminal Procedure (Insanity and Unfitness to Plead) Bill: Briefing on the Private Member's Bill.* London: The Law Society Legal Practice Directorate.

MacFarlane, P. J. M. (1987). Unfitness to be tried for an offence. *Criminal Law Journal, 11,* 67–77.

Mackay, R. D. (1990). Insanity and fitness to stand trial in Canada and England: A comparative study. *Journal of Forensic Psychiatry, 1*, 277–303.

Mackay, R. D. (1991). The decline of disability in relation to trial. *Criminal Law Review*, 87–97.

Manson, A. (1982). Fit to be tried: Unravelling the knots. *Queen's Law Journal, 7*, 305–343.

Maxson, L. S., & Neuringer, C. (1970). Evaluating legal competency. *Journal of Genetic Psychology, 117*, 267–273.

McGarry, A. L. (1971). The fate of psychotic offenders returned for trial. *American Journal of Psychiatry, 127*, 1181–1184.

Menzies, R. L., Webster, C. D., Butler, B. T., & Turner, R. E. (1980). The outcome of forensic psychiatric assessment: A study of remands in six Canadian cities. *Criminal Justice and Behaviour, 7*, 471–480.

Miller, R. D., & Germain, E. J. (1987). Evaluation of competency to stand trial in defendants who do not want to be defended against the crimes charged. *Bulletin of the American Academy of Psychiatry and the Law, 15*, 371–379.

Mitchell, S., & Richardson, P. J. (1985). *Archbold - Pleading, evidence and practice in criminal cases* (42nd ed.). London: Sweet and Maxwell.

Mowbray, C. T. (1979). A study of patients treated as incompetent to stand trial. *Social Psychiatry, 14*, 31–39.

Nicholson, R. A., & Johnson, W. G. (1991). Prediction of competency to stand trial: Contribution of demographics, type of offense, clinical characteristics, and psycholegal ability. *International Journal of Law and Psychiatry, 14*, 287–297.

Normand, A. C. (1984). Unfitness for trial in Scotland: Proposed adjudication of the facts and the right to reprosecute. *International Journal of Law and Psychiatry, 7*, 415–435.

Pendleton, L. (1980). Treatment of persons found incompetent to stand trial. *American Journal of Psychiatry, 137*, 1098–1100.

Phillips, M. R., Wolf, A. S., & Coons, D. J. (1988). Psychiatry and the criminal justice system: Testing the myths. *American Journal of Psychiatry, 145*, 605–610.

Pike, L. O. (1873, 1876). *A history of crime in England, illustrating the changes of the laws in the progress of civilisation* (Vols i & ii). London: Smith, Elder & Co.

Poole, A. R. (1968). Standing mute and fitness to plead. *Criminal Law Review*, 6–23.

Prevezer, S. (1958). Fitness to plead and the Criminal Lunatics Act, 1800. *Criminal Law Review*, 144–153.

Rachlin, S., Stokman, C. L. J., & Grossman, S. (1986). Incompetent misdemeanants - pseudocivil commitment. *Bulletin of the American Academy of Psychiatry and the Law, 14*, 23–30.

Rappeport, J. R., Conti, N. P., & Rudnick, B. (1983). A new pretrial screening program. *Bulletin of the American Academy of Psychiatry and the Law, 11*, 239–248.

Richardson, H. G. & Sayles, G. O. (1966). *Law and legislation from Aethelberht to Magna Carta*. Edinburgh University Press.

Robey, A. (1965). Criteria for competency to stand trial: A checklist for psychiatrists. *American Journal of Psychiatry, 122*, 616–622.

Roesch, R. (1979). Determining competency to stand trial: An examination of evaluation procedures in an institutional setting. *Journal of Consulting and Clinical Psychology, 47*, 542–550.

Roesch, R., Eaves, D., Sollner, R., Normandin, M., & Glackman, W. (1981). Evaluating fitness to stand trial: A comparative analysis of fit and unfit defendants. *International Journal of Law and Psychiatry, 4*, 145–157.

Roesch, R., Jackson, M. A., Sollner, R., Eaves, D., Glackman, W., & Webster, C. D. (1984). The fitness to stand trial interview test: How four professions rate videotaped fitness interviews. *International Journal of Law and Psychiatry, 7*, 115–131.

Royal Commission on Capital Punishment. (1953). *1949–1953: Report.* London: HMSO.

Schreiber, J. (1982). Professional judgement in the assessment of competency to stand trial: Report of an evaluation study. *International Journal of Law and Psychiatry, 5*, 331–340.

Schreiber, J., Roesch, R., & Golding, S. (1987). An evaluation of procedures for assessing competency to stand trial. *Bulletin of the American Academy of Psychiatry and the Law, 15*, 187–203.

Scottish Home and Health Department and Crown Office. (1975). *Criminal Procedure in Scotland, Second Report (The Thomson Committee)*, cmnd. 6218. Edinburgh: HMSO.

Siegel, A. M., & Elwork, A. (1990). Treating incompetence to stand trial. *Law and Human Behavior, 14*, 57–65.

SPSS Inc. (1983). *SPSS-X user's guide.* Chicago: McGraw-Hill.

SPSS Inc. (1988). *SPSS-PC+ V2.0 base manual.* Chicago: SPSS Inc.

Steadman, H. J., Monahan, J., Hartstone, E., Davis, S. K., & Robbins, P. C. (1982). Mentally disordered offenders: A national survey of patients and facilities. *Law and Human Behavior, 6*, 31–38.

Szasz, T. S. (1968). *Psychiatric justice.* New York: Macmillan.

Turner, R. V. (1968). *The king and his courts: The role of John and Henry III in the administration of justice 1199–1240.* Ithaca, NY: Cornell University Press.

Verdun-Jones, S. N. (1981). The doctrine of fitness to stand trial in Canada: The forked tongue of social control. *International Journal of Law and Psychiatry, 4*, 363–389.

Walker, N. (1968). *Crime and insanity in England, Vol. 1: The historical perspective.* Edinburgh University Press.

Walker, N., & McCabe, S. (1973). *Crime and insanity in England, Vol 2: New solutions and new problems.* Edinburgh University Press.

Warren, J. I., Fitch, W. L., Dietz, P. E., & Rosenfeld, B.D. (1991). Criminal offense psychiatric diagnosis, and psycholegal opinion: An analysis of 894 Pretrial referrals. *Bulletin of the American Academy of Psychiatry and the Law, 19*, 63–69.

White, S. (1992). The Criminal Procedure (Insanity and Unfitness to Plead). Act. *Criminal Law Review*, 4–14.

Wood, P. J. W., & Guly, O. C. R. (1991). Unfit to plead to murder: Three case reports. *Medicine, Science and the Law, 31*, 55–60.

CASES
England

Proceedings in the Case of John Frith, for High Treason, at Justice Hall in the Old Bailey, on Saturday, April 17th: 30 George III (1790). Howell's State Trials, Vol. 22 (1783–1794). 308.

R v *Benyon* [1957] 2 Q.B. 111.
R v *Berry* (1876). 1 Q.B.D 447.
R v *Berry* (1977). Cr App R 156.
R v *Dyson* (1831). 7 C .& P. 305,n.
R v *Davies* (1853). C.L.C. 326.
R v *Jelen and Katz* (1990). Cr. App. R. 456.
R v *Governor of H.M. Prison at Stafford, ex p Emery* [1909] 2 K.B. 81.
R v *Podola* (1959). Cr. App. R. 220.
R v *Pritchard* (1836).   7 C. & P. 303.
R v *Roberts* [1953] 2 All E. R. 340.
R v *Robertson* [1968] 3 All E. R. 557.
R v *Samuel* (1987). Cr. App. R. 232.
R v *Sharp* [1958] 1 All E. R. 62.
R v. *Steel* (1787). 2 Leach 507.
R v *Thomas Jones* (1773). 1 Leach 102.
R v *Turton* (1854). 6 Cox, C.C. 385.
R v *Vent* (1935). 25 Cr. App. R. 55.
R v *Webb* [1969] 2 All E. R.

United States
Dusky v *United States* (1960). 362 US 402.
Jackson v *Indiana* (1972). 406 US 715.

Author index

Jackson, M. A., 42
Jackson v Indiana, 26, 37
James, K., 85, 86, 87, 88, 92, 95
Johnson, W. G., 40
Johnston, N., 40, 45(n)

Kunjukrishnan, R., 40

Lamb, H. R., 38, 39
Larkin, E. P., 3, 33–34
Law Society, 25, 96
Lister, E.D., 39, 40

MacFarlane, P. J. M., 27
Mackay, R. D., 34, 41
Manson, A., 15, 22
Maxson, L. S., 42
McCabe, S., 53, 86, 87, 95
McGarry, A. L., 37
Menzies, R. L., 40
Miller, R. D., 39
Mitchell, S., 2
Monahan, J., 26, 37, 39
Mowbray, C. T., 38, 39

Neuringer, C., 42
Nicholson, R. A., 40
Normand, A. C., 3, 27, 28, 35, 36
Normandin, M., 41

Pendleton, L., 26, 29(n), 43
Phillips, M. R., 39, 40, 42
Pike, L. O., 10, 11
Pogany, E., 40, 45(n)
Poole, A. R., 11, 19, 25, 28
Prevezer, S., 17
Proceedings in the Case of John
   Frith, for High Treason, 13

R v *Benyon*, 19
R v *Berry* (1876), 17
R v *Berry* (1977), 20–21
R v *Davies*, 17
R v *Dyson*, 1, 15
R v *Governor of H.M. Prison at
   Stafford.*, 18
R v *Jelen and Katz.*, 106
R v *Podola*, 20, 21
R v *Pritchard*, 2, 16

R v *Roberts*, 19
R v *Robertson*, 20, 90, 111
R v *Samuel*, 106
R v *Sharp*, 20
R v. Steel, 12
R v *Thomas Jones.*, 12
R v *Turton*, 20
R v *Vent*, 20
R v *Webb*, 1
Rachlin, S., 39
Randolph, J. J., 41
Rappeport, J. R., 40
Richardson, H. G., 6
Richardson, P. J., 2
Robbins, P. C., 26, 37, 39
Robertson, G., 85, 86, 87, 88, 92, 95
Robey, A., 42
Roesch, R., 26, 28, 39, 41, 42
Rosenfeld, B.D., 39, 40
Royal Commission on Capital
   Punishment., 23, 29(n), 31
Rudnick, B., 40

Sayles, G. O., 6
Schreiber, J., 42
Scottish Home and Health
   Department and Crown Office,
   27, 28, 29(n), 94
Siegel, A. M., 43
Sollner, R., 41, 42
SPSS Inc., 48
Steadman, H. J., 26, 37, 39
Stokman, C. L. J., 39
Szasz, T. S., 39

Taliana, L. E., 41
Thomas, H. E., 37, 42, 90
Turner, R. E., 40
Turner, R. V., 7

Verdun-Jones, S. N., 28, 39, 41

Walker, N., 5, 6, 7–9, 12, 13, 14, 18,
   23, 25, 29(n), 31, 52, 53, 86, 87, 95
Warren, J. I., 39, 40
Webster, C. D., 40, 42
White, S., 25, 91, 105, 106
Wolf, A. S., 39, 40, 42
Wood, P. J. W., 33

Subject index

FORTHCOMING MONOGRAPHS

AGGRESSION, INDIVIDUAL DIFFERENCES, ALCOHOL AND BENZODIAZEPINES

Alyson Bond, Malcolm Lader, José Carlos C. da Silveira

THE RAPIST

Donald Grubin and John Gunn

THE DRUG TRANSITION STUDIES

Changes in Route of Administration of Heroin and Cocaine for Populations and Individuals

John Strang, Michael Gossop

PSYCHOSIS IN THE INNER CITY

David Castle, Simon Wessely, Jim Van Os, Robin Murray

For more information, please contact:

The Promotions Department
Psychology Press
27 Church Road, Hove
East Sussex, (UK) BN3 2FA
Tel: +44 (0) 1273 207 411   Fax: +44 (0) 1273 205 612